MEDITERRANEAN DIET COOKBOOK FOR BEGINNERS

1500 Days of Easy & Delicious Mediterranean Recipes for Getting Started Eating Well Every Day | 28-Days Meal Plan to Help You Create a New Healthy Lifestyle

BY

ELENA WILSON

Table of Contents

Introduction

Our diet has a direct impact on both our physical and mental health as well as how long we live. This Mediterranean cookbook for beginners can be useful whether you're just learning to cook, beginning your transition to a healthier diet, or trying to streamline your routine.

The Mediterranean diet is more of an approach to eating than a set of rules about what you can and can't consume. Its objective is to include the wholesome foods that people often eat in the Mediterranean region. In addition to healthy nutrients like nuts & olive oil, it's loaded with fish, entire grains, fruits, veggies, beans, as well as lentils. While avoiding red meat, sweets, and processed meals, it also contains a reasonable amount of chicken, turkey, eggs, and fermented dairy products like yogurt or kefir. The diet also stresses the value of preparing meals at home, sharing meals with people, and getting regular exercise, like walking.

The main components of the genuine Mediterranean diet are: a high intake of whole, fresh foods; a low intake of processed foods, high-calorie proteins, and starchy or refined carbs; and a moderate dose of wine. Exercising daily, socializing, and eating meals with people go beyond the fundamental idea of eating wholesome and delicious foods. These integrated dietary practices support the development of a better understanding of the joys of wholesome eating and contentment.

The eating plan will not only improve your mental and physical health, but also your general moods and emotions because it encourages you to eat healthful meals. You will become a happier and more fulfilled person if you take everything in moderation and avoid taking too much of a good thing. The Mediterranean Diet focuses on restoring your health by eating and living sensibly so that your life is forever changed for the better.

This manual aims to provide you a thorough understanding of the subject and all of its facets. Additionally, this book includes the bulk of the recipes that are typically suggested in studies showing that this is a healthy way to eat as well as the 28-day diet meal plan.

Let's dive in for more information!

Chapter 1

Fundamentals of the Mediterranean diet

What is the Mediterranean diet?

The phrase "Mediterranean diet" refers to a broad range of traditional eating practices in the nations that border the Mediterranean Sea. There isn't a single, accepted Mediterranean diet. The Mediterranean is bordered by at least 16 nations. Due to cultural differences, ethnic heritage, religion, economy, geography, and agricultural production, eating habits vary between various countries and even within each country's regions. However, there are some commonalities.

Included in a typical Mediterranean diet are:

- vegetables, fruits, grains, tubers, beans, nuts, seeds, and nut butter in voluminous supply;
- Fat sources are mostly fats
- Low to moderate amounts of chicken, fish, eggs, and dairy products.

In this diet, fish & poultry are more prevalent than red meat. Additionally, plant-based foods with little processing are the main focus. Low to moderate amounts of wine can be drunk, usually with meals. As opposed to desserts, fruit is frequently served.

Explanation

There is a 99.9% chance that you have heard of the Mediterranean diet if you are interested in healthy living. You have most likely already done it or are doing it right now. Regardless, the foundation of this diet is the traditional cuisine of nations like Greece and Italy. Ancel Benjamin Keys, a physiologist, and his wife are credited with popularizing it.

Keys and his team conducted an extensive study on the benefits of the Mediterranean diet for human health in the 1960s. In the course of fifty years, he produced several researches that involved seven nations: Italy, Greece, Finland, the Netherlands, Tokyo, Yugoslavia, as well as the United States.

In contrast to men from other nations, he found that men from Greece, and particularly Crete, had lower incidences of heart disease. Keys came to the conclusion that a diet high in fruits and vegetables was directly responsible for the much decreased rate of heart issues.

The Mediterranean diet changed over time, but most of the changes were slight, thus it mostly remained the same. A Mediterranean diet consists primarily of fruits and vegetables, but it also contains significant amounts of whole grains, nuts, legumes, seeds, fish, shellfish, spices, herbs, and olive oil.

The diet suggests consuming modest amounts of eggs, chicken, cheese, and yogurt along with very little red meat. It is quite restrictive when it comes to sugar and discourages the intake of refined carbohydrates, added sugars, and sugar-sweetened beverages. Additionally, it limits the consumption of refined oil-containing foods, highly processed foods, and processed meat.

Components of the Mediterranean diet

Local foods found in the Mediterranean regions, such as wheat, olive trees, and vineyards, serve as the basis for the essential components of the Mediterranean diet.

Almond oil

Due to its lower fatty acid content and high antioxidant and anti-inflammatory qualities, olive oil is a mainstay in many Mediterranean diets. Its three main manufacturers worldwide are Greece, Spain, and Italy. The main source of fat in Mediterranean cuisine is olive oil, which is also used for baking in addition to cooking.

Wheat

Wheat is another essential component of Mediterranean cuisine; it is high in fibre and has a low glycemic index. Farro, ancient wheat, was traditionally processed with millstones to create flour. Making couscous, pasta, and bread all frequently employ unrefined wheat and barley flour.

Wild kale

In Greece and other Mediterranean countries, greens are essential elements in baked savory dishes. Among the wild greens are dandelions, chicory, and fennel. The omega-3 fatty acids found in greens are quite beneficial.

Wine

Although wine is frequently consumed during meals in the Mediterranean diet, it is done so in moderation. Consumption of red wine is on the rise because of its health benefits, including its ability to increase good cholesterol while decreasing badly.

Olives

Another good source of antioxidants is olives, particularly kalamata olives. They are employed in the preparation and flavoring of Mediterranean cuisine.

Chickpeas

One of the earliest types of legumes, chickpeas is a staple in Mediterranean cuisine. Chickpeas are high in protein, potassium, iron, and fibre. It is either made into flour or used to make hummus.

Nuts

The Mediterranean diet includes nuts because they are abundant in healthful fats. Nuts are high in calories, thus eating them in moderation is recommended.

Herbs

Greek food requires flavanol, which is provided by herbs. Although herbs differ from place to region, they are crucial to the meals of the Mediterranean. They include antioxidants and anti-inflammatory substances.

Cheese and yogurt with feta

Yogurt and feta cheese add additional protein and lipids to a plant-based Mediterranean diet. Yogurt and feta were traditionally fermented, which increases their probiotic content. A typical Greek breakfast consists of yogurt with honey, fresh berries, and cheese, along with greens and cherry tomato halves.

The Mediterranean diet Pyramid

As a child, you probably learned about the food pyramid, which lists all the many nutrition groups in ascending order of importance. The most significant group was at the bottom of the pyramid, followed by the least significant group at the top.

If you recall, the bottom category of the food pyramid you learned about in school was bread. However, there is another chart that may be useful to consult. The Mediterranean diet, which has numerous benefits supported by science and is rated the best diet for general health, has its own food pyramid.

The Mediterranean diet pyramid can be used as a roadmap for adhering to a Mediterranean diet because it represents the traditional lifestyle and dietary components of nations that border the Mediterranean Sea. The items that you ought to eat daily and include in each meal make up the pyramid's base. Olive oil, fresh produce, healthy grains, beans, lentils, nuts, and olives are all part of this diet.

Second-tier foods are those you should eat at least once a week, such as fish and seafood. The foods to eat in moderation come next. Poultry, eggs, cheese, yogurt, and, occasionally, red wine are among them. Last but not least, the Mediterranean diet's smallest serving—usually reserved for special occasions—includes red meat, saturated fats, and occasional sweets.

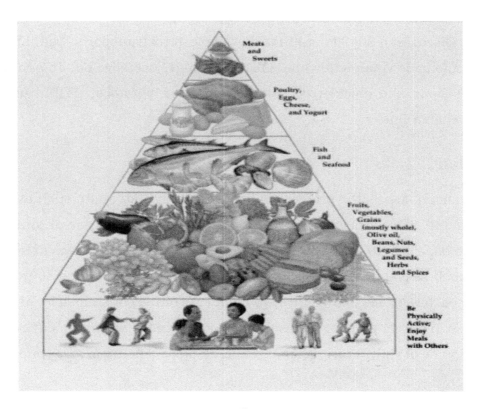

Exercise and the idea of sharing meals with others are also included in the Mediterranean diet pyramid as essential elements of a healthy living. It is beneficial to include these elements because a healthy diet cannot make up for insufficient exercise, and the opposite is also true. Additionally, "eating with people and sharing meals are some of the oldest ways to connect and strengthen bonds with friends and family. It also frequently encourages more thoughtful, even slower eating than eating alone.

Life key Habits of feeling Healthier than ever with the Mediterranean diet

Start small if changing your entire approach to eating and shopping seems difficult. It may not be necessary or sustainable to start over from scratch. Here, we provide a list of actions you may do to transition your diet to a more Mediterranean one. Pick one of the tactics listed below, and practice it often. When you're prepared, switch to the following tactic. These eight suggestions for beginning a Mediterranean diet might help you enjoy the health advantages regardless of where you decide to start.

Cook with olive oil first

Consider transitioning to extra-virgin olive oil if you have been cooking using vegetable or coconut oil. Olive oil's high concentration of polyunsaturated fatty acids has been linked to increased levels of HDL cholesterol. An investigation published in Nutrition, Metabolism & Cardiovascular Diseases in 2019 found that HDL cholesterol transports "bad" LDL particles from arteries. For homemade vinaigrettes and salad dressings, use olive oil. To add flavor, drizzle it over completed foods like chicken or fish. For mashed potatoes, pasta, and other dishes, substitutes olive oil or butter.

Consume fish

In the Mediterranean, fish is the primary source of protein. Fatty fish, such as trout, sardines, especially mackerel, play a crucial role in this diet. The omega-3 fatty acids found in abundance in these fish are beneficial to cardiovascular and neurological health. Even fish with less fat and thinner flesh, such as cod or tilapia, are worthwhile since they are a rich source of protein. Set aside one night each week as "fish night" if you don't currently consume a lot of fish in your diet. One easy and clean way to prepare dinner is to cook fish in foil or parchment paper packets. Or try adding it to some of your favorite dishes, such as tacos, stir-fries, and soups.

Consume vegetables all day.

This is the ideal time to add additional vegetables to your diet if you're concerned that there aren't enough of them in it. Eating one serving at snack time, such as munching on bell pepper strips or blending up some spinach for a smoothie, and one serving at dinner, such as these quick and simple side dishes, is an excellent way to accomplish this. Aim for two servings or more per day. According to Australian studies, more is better—at least three meals can reduce stress.

Take a handful of Whole Grains

Try "genuine" whole grains that aren't refined and are still in their "whole" state. Quinoa is an excellent side dish for weekday meals because it cooks in less than 20 minutes. Barley is nourishing and high in fibre; combine it with mushrooms for a hearty, savory soup. A warm cup of oats is perfect for a winter morning breakfast. Even caramel is a whole grain; all you need to do is consume air-popped popcorn and skip the buttery to keep it healthy. Start eating more whole-grain items like pasta and bread.

Food packaging and ingredient lists should prominently feature the words "whole" or "pretty much the entire grain" as the very first item. To gradually introduce a whole grain, use whole-grain pastas and rice or combine a whole grain half-and-half with a refined one, such as half-whole-wheat pasta and half-white pasta, if switching from your previous refined faves is still too difficult for you.

Enjoy Some Nuts

Another component of the Mediterranean diet is nuts. Whether it is almonds, cashews, or pistachios, grabbing a handful can make for a filling on-the-go snack. Almonds are a healthier alternative to common snack foods including cookies, fries, crisps, snacking mix, and cereal bars, as shown in a study released in Nutrition Journal. Nuts also have more fibre and mineral contents than processed snack foods, such as potassium. Rather than salted, glazed, or chocolate-coated nuts, opt for unsalted and unsweetened varieties.

Indulge in fruit as dessert

Fruits are a rich source of fiber, vitamin C, and phytonutrients, making them an excellent addition to any diet. They are the ideal dessert or snack to save your sweet taste. If adding a little sugar makes you want to eat more, try drizzling honey on pear slices or brown sugar on grapefruit. Keep fresh fruit on display at home and bring a piece or two with you to work so you may have a healthy snack whenever your tummy grumbles. Many supermarkets also carry exotic fruit; choose a new variety to sample each week and broaden your fruit horizons.

Have a glass of wine

Although the inhabitants of the Mediterranean region, including the Spanish, Italians, French, Greeks, and others, are not considered to be wine snobs, this does not mean that you should pour wine whenever you choose. Dietitians and other specialists who created the Mediterranean diet for the New England Journal of Medicine study suggested that women limit their daily serving sizes to 3-ounces and men to 5-ounces. Try to drink whenever you eat a meal; it's even better if you eat it with close friends or family. If you don't drink, you shouldn't start doing so solely to follow this diet.

Enjoy Each Bite

Eating in the Mediterranean style is a lifestyle choice as well as a diet. Instead of eating hastily in front of the television, take the time to savor the company of your loved ones while you leisurely consume your meal at the table. Eating slowly will not only make you appreciate your meal and the company of others, but it will also help you become more aware of your body's hunger and fullness cues. When you are satisfied with your meal, you are more likely to quit eating than when you are bursting at the seams with food.

How Does This Diet Works?

There is no formal way to follow the Mediterranean diet because it was never established as a weight-loss plan in the first place. Instead, it is a way of eating that has naturally formed over time in a particular region of people. But because it takes a balanced, unrestrictive attitude to food, it is widespread. Ikaria, which is located in Greece, and Sardinia, which is located in Italy, are two of the four blue zones, which are regions where people are living longer and are less likely to become sick. Both of these cities are located in the Mediterranean. These regions are thought to have some of the lowest incidences of cancer and heart disease in the entire world.

Because this is a dining habit rather than a diet, you can see how many calories you can consume to lose or weight maintenance, what you can do to be healthier, and how your Mediterranean cuisine will be prepared. Maintain the Mediterranean diet pyramid.

The food groups highlighted in this pyramid include fruit, vegetables, pretty much entire grains, beans, legumes, olive oil, aromatic herbs, and spices. Fish and seafood, as well as reasonable portions of poultry, egg, cheese, and dairy, should be ingested at least a couple of times per week. Candy and red meat should only be consumed on special occasions. Finish with a splash of red wine (if you like), keep moving, and you're finished.

If your doctor says you don't need two glasses a day for males and one for women, that's great. Resveratrol, which appears to lengthen life, has made red wine better, but hundreds or thousands of glasses need to be consumed to make an impact.

What Is the Cost of the Mediterranean Diet?

Like most other parts of the diet, the expense of the Mediterranean diet relies on how it is planned. Although some items, including olive oil, fruits, seafood, or fresh foods, can be pricey, some research suggests there are methods to reduce the cost, especially if you substitute home-cooked plant-based meals for meals that often contain red meat. Your purchasing preferences matter a lot. The $50 bottle of wine should spring, right? Take one for $15 instead. On that particular day, $3 worth of vegetables are sold in place of the artichokes.

What advantages does this diet have for your health?

Here is a comprehensive list of all the health advantages of following the Mediterranean diet lifestyle.

Lowers Your Heart Disease Risk

The Mediterranean diet is renowned for being heart-healthy, if there is one thing. It thus consistently obtains favorable reviews from U.S. News & Report in the categories of Best Overall Diet and Best Heart-Healthy Diet.

It's obvious why:

The claim that the Mediterranean diet is excellent for your heart is supported by a ton of scientific data.

As fact, a 2016 study involving and over 20,000 adults found that people who follow the Mediterranean diet have a considerably lower risk of developing heart disease. The researchers even proposed that adopting a Mediterranean diet could prevent up to 4% of all cases of heart disease (Tong et al., 2016).

Another study compared those who followed a Mediterranean diet to those who did not to see which group was at a higher risk of heart attack, stroke, and mortality from cardiovascular causes. The study, which lasted almost five years, found that those who ate a Mediterranean diet had risks that were almost 30% lower (Rosato et al., 2019).

If you're still not satisfied that the Mediterranean diet is heart-healthy, have a look at this 2019 review of the literature that looked at 29 different studies on the topic. The authors of the review concluded that the Healthy eating guards against several cardiac diseases (Rosato et al., 2019).

May Delay Cognitive Aging

According to some research, eating a Mediterranean-style diet may reduce cognitive decline and fend against degenerative conditions like Alzheimer's disease. Even though further research is necessary, the current findings are unquestionably encouraging!

For example, a meta-analysis of 12 studies on the Mediterranean diet and its effects on brain health was published in the journal Frontiers in Nutrition in 2016. The review concluded that there is "encouraging evidence that increased people who adhere to a Mediterranean diet is linked with enhancing learning and memory, going to slow cognitive decline, or reducing the transition to Alzheimer's disease" (Lourida et al., 2013)

A 2015 study especially examined the impact of the MIND diet, which combines the DASH Diet and the Mediterranean Diet. According to research, this diet "significantly reduces cognitive decline" (Morris et al., 2015). Early studies on the Mediterranean diet and conditions like Alzheimer's should not be used to draw any firm conclusions, but it appears that the majority of specialists concur that the Mediterranean diet and its variations, such as the MIND diet, can enhance brain function.

May Facilitate Weight Loss

The Mediterranean diet is an option to explore if you want to lose weight. According to research, the Mediterranean diet can aid in weight loss and weight maintenance. It has been demonstrated that the Mediterranean diet can aid in weight loss almost as effectively as a low-carb diet (Shai et al.,2008).

Additionally, a significant 2018 study (with over 32,000 individuals) discovered that eating a Mediterranean-style diet lowers the risk for abdominal obesity (Agnoli et al., 2018). Slower weight loss at the advised rate of one to two pounds per week is often more maintainable than rapid weight loss over a short period of time.

Is it possible to reduce a Stroke?

In the same study in which they determined that a Mediterranean diet might save up to 6% of cases of coronary disease, researchers found that it could save up to 8.5% of stroke cases (Tong et al., 2016). Additionally, a 2018 study from the UK discovered that eating a Mediterranean-style diet considerably lowers the risk of having a stroke (Paterson et al., 2018). However, the study's authors point out that this finding only held true for women, not men, and that this merits additional study.

Research findings are sometimes accurate in one place but not in another, however, the association between the Mediterranean diet and lower risk of stroke appears to be widespread: Over 15,000 patients in 39 countries were tracked for nearly four years as part of a 2016 study published in the European Heart Journal. The patients' degree of adherence to the Mediterranean diet was directly correlated with the degree to which their risk of suffering a heart attack, stroke, or passing away due to cardiovascular reasons was reduced (Ralph et al., 2016).

In high-risk individuals, switching to and maintaining a Mediterranean diet might prevent up to 30 percent of cardiac arrest, strokes, and lives lost from heart disease. This study, published in the New England Medical Journal in 2013, may be the most heartening link between both the Mediterranean diet as well as stroke risk.

It may seem strange that a diet that prioritizes carb-rich foods like pasta and ancient grains might aid in the management or prevention of type 2 diabetes.

- The Mediterranean diet places an emphasis on eating whole grains and carbohydrates derived from vegetables since these types of carbohydrates have a less detrimental effect on blood sugar levels than processed carbs do.
- The diet also contains a lot of protein and good fats.
- Too many desserts and sweets are discouraged by the diet.
- The Mediterranean way of life promotes regular exercise, which aids in the control of diabetes.

Adopting a Mediterranean diet may reduce the chance of developing diabetes by as much as 19 percent, according to the findings of a review of nine distinct studies that was published in 2014. The investigations were conducted in 2014. These findings were supported by a 2020 study that found a stronger adherence to the Mediterranean diet is associated with a lower incidence of type 2-diabetes (Georgoulis et al., 2014).

May Be Beneficial for Arthritis Patients

There is some evidence that the Mediterranean diet may help arthritis sufferers feel less pain. The Mediterranean diet has many anti-inflammatory foods, which makes sense given that arthritis is an inflammatory disease. The Mediterranean diet includes wholesome anti-inflammatory foods like berries, olive oil, and dark green vegetables, according to the Arthritis Foundation, which supports it as a means of managing arthritis.

Could Prevent Some Cancers

The protection provided by the Mediterranean diet against chronic illnesses like diabetes, coronary heart disease, and metabolic syndrome is well-known and lauded. It turns out that this anti-inflammatory and antioxidant-rich diet may also offer protection from some malignancies.

Eating a Mediterranean diet may protect against cancers of the breast, stomach, liver, prostate, and head and neck, according to a 2017 analysis of studies (Schwingshackl et al., 2017). The preventive benefit is "primarily driven by larger diets of fruits, veggies, and whole grains," the scientists note.

In a separate study conducted in 2015, researchers examined the efficacy of a Mediterranean diet and a low-fat diet in warding against breast cancer in female participants. Some research suggests that following a Mediterranean diet, particularly one that incorporates extra virgin olive oil as a dietary supplement, can help reduce the risk of breast cancer development (Toledo et al., 2015).

Lower LDL and BP

LDL cholesterol, also known as "bad" cholesterol, and blood pressure are two crucial indicators of your health and the likelihood of developing various ailments. When either marker is elevated, it may be a sign of a health issue or an issue in and of itself.

The Mediterranean diet is one of the many options available for controlling and lowering LDL cholesterol and blood pressure. In order to understand how the diets of over 800 firemen affected various health markers, experts assessed their diets in 2014.

They discovered that the more closely the guys followed a Mediterranean diet, the healthier their cholesterol levels (Yang et al., 2014). Although more research is required to completely understand how the Mediterranean diet affects blood pressure, it can lower blood pressure in both those with and without hypertension.

Diet preferences accommodated

Vegans, vegetarianism, paleos, gluten-free, lactose, and others can thrive on the Mediterranean diet. You can modify the diet to your liking. Diet works best when all food groups are allowed.

The Mediterranean diet includes plenty of carbs, proteins, essential fats, fruits, vegetables, and even certain delights in moderation (calling all red wine fans!).

The Mediterranean diet advocates consuming foods from Mediterranean regions. Without a focus on restriction, these foods and diversity improve health, but if this eating style is turned into a rigorous weight loss strategy, detrimental dieting effects may be experienced.

Promotes Exercise

The Mediterranean diet is one of the few eating plans that specifically encourage physical exercise. Given that the majority of adults in America don't exercise enough, this is a good addition. Additionally, frequent exercisers are more likely to choose healthier meals throughout the day.

In contrast to the typical diet consumed in Western countries, the consumption of foods from the Mediterranean region has been shown in a recent study to be associated with improved levels of physical performance. This gives rise to the possibility that the connection between physical activity and the Mediterranean diet is a two-way street (Baker et al., 2019).

Places a focus on moderation and variety

The fact that the Mediterranean diet allows for a wide variety of foods and flavors means you won't become bored or feel confined, which is one major reason why it may be so helpful for long-term weight loss. The Mediterranean diet is an excellent choice if you frequently yo-yo between restrictive and non-restrictive eating patterns because you can still enjoy rich flavors, carb-heavy foods, and even chocolate and wine.

Additionally, even if you are in a caloric deficit, hunger shouldn't be a problem because the Mediterranean diet prioritizes foods that are high in protein and fibre. Whole grains, nuts, cheese, and fish are examples of foods that help you stay satiated longer. Additionally, you'll be cooking with satiety-increasing healthy fats like olive oil.

Why should you start the Mediterranean diet?

Creating a sustainable meal plan for consuming more Mediterranean-style meals is your ultimate objective. You have a dozen minor steps to pick from as soon as you make the transition. Eventually, make your choice a habit.

- Take another step once your tactical decision has become ingrained in your eating habit and you feel ready to proceed. Whichever stage you decide to start with, each one will encourage you to start a proper program performance with the Mediterranean Diet and enjoy the benefits of the diet. The wise many that have made the changeover to this eating style frequently state collectively that they will no longer eat in any other way.

- Long-term adherence to a Mediterranean diet shouldn't be a problem because it doesn't cut out any whole food groupings.

- The Mediterranean diet may be excellent. You may create something that will transport you over the Atlantic with the right recipe and wine. The user-friendly advice makes food preparation and planning easier. You can dine out as long as you have a companion to share heavier items with.

- The Mediterranean diet allows you to cook and store food ahead of time, but if you have more time than money, you'll need to employ a cook to plan, shop for, and prepare your meals.

- There is a lot of information in the manual, including an understandable food pyramid, detailed advice on the Mediterranean transition, and simple recipes.

- With this diet, you shouldn't experience hunger because it is full of delicious fats and fiber-rich foods like whole grains. You will also cook with pleasing fats like olive oil. Nutritionists place a high value on satiety, or the sense of relaxation.

- You are in charge of everything, and you are aware of the responsibility for any poor quality.

- If you have a sensible plan, there are very few health risks associated with the Mediterranean diet. Everyone, from young children and adults to the elderly, can safely use the method. However, before making significant dietary changes, healthy individuals should consult their doctor.

What to Eat and What to Avoid

Free eating

Veggies - Whether they are stir-fried, steamed, baked, grilled, pickled, or raw, fill your plate with healthy, vibrant vegetables. Greens, onions, shallots, leeks, celery, cloves, ginger, yam, sweet potatoes, root crops, turnips, cabbage, broccoli, Brussel sprouts, beets, tomatoes, artichoke, eggplants, peppers, etc. are among the veggies you can eat. Your preferred vegetables can be added to a salad, scrambled eggs, or pizza.

Fruits - Include fiber- and antioxidant-rich fruits like apples, avocados, bananas, berries, figs, apricots, grapes, olives, oranges, pears, melons, and peaches in your diet. Eat as many fruits as you can, from those that are seasonal to those that are cultivated locally. And only consume fruits after dinner or lunch or when you are seeking sugar.

Healthy Grains: Grains are rich in fibre and anti-oxidants. Whole grains like oats, brown rice, maize, Farro, couscous, sorghum, bulgur, and buckwheat are permitted on the Mediterranean diet. Also, choose whole-grain alternatives for your bread and pasta.

Proteins - Include a variety of lean proteins in your meal plan, such as fish such as salmon, trout, sardines, anchovies, oysters, mackerel, shrimp, mussels, crab, clams, and shellfish that are high in omega-3 fatty acids. You can also receive plant-based protein from nuts, seeds, beans, and legumes like almonds, peanuts, walnuts, hazelnuts, cashews, pumpkin seeds, chia seeds, sesame seeds, and pulses like beans, lentils, peas, and chickpeas. Include them in your salads or eat them on their own as snacks.

Olive oil can be used to prepare food, make sauces, baked goods, make vinaigrettes for salads, and a lot more. Other types of healthy oils that you can use include safflower, canola, and peanut oils.

Water: By drinking lemonade or sparkling water, you can flavor the water. You can also have one serving of red wine each day. Drinking wine lowers bad cholesterol, reduces stress, and enhances food flavors. Also acceptable are unsweetened tea and coffee.

Eat-in moderation

Fish and shellfish should be your primary choices for protein. However, you can also choose dairy products like Greek yogurt, cheese, and eggs, as well as fowl like chicken, duck, and turkey.

Fats: Additional sources of fat include full-fat cheeses like parmesan, coconut cream, nut butters, almond butter, etc.

Rarely eating

Red meat: Red meat is occasionally allowed on the Mediterranean diet. Additionally, only cook organic, grass-fed meats like beef, lamb, hog, and others. Steer clear of processed and raw meats.

Avoid

Foods that have been highly processed should not be purchased, even if they bear the designation "low-fat."

Avoid refined grains, such as white flour, whole wheat flour, and others, while making pasta and bread.

Refined oil - The Mediterranean diet strongly forbids the consumption of unhealthy oils like canola oil, soybean oil, and others.

Tran's fats: The Mediterranean diet strictly prohibits Tran's fats. Margarine & processed foods contain them.

The Mediterranean diet forbids added sugar, which includes table sugar and sugar found in ice cream, candy, soda, fruit juices, sugar drinks, and other products. Natural sugar is the only type of sugar that is permitted.

Avoid processed meats, such as hot dogs, processed sausages, etc., which are not organic, grass-fed, or pasture-raised.

Some Food-Related Important Notes

Given that there are so many different types of food in so many different nations, there is some debate over the specific items that should be consumed as part of the Mediterranean diet. The primary lesson is that there isn't a complete list. In light of this, you should consume more naturally occurring plant-based foods than animal-based foods in your diet.

Additionally, it's advised to consume fish at least twice weekly and to abstain from beef at least one day a week. Exercise, eating meals together as a family and general happiness are some further aspects of the Mediterranean lifestyle not everything is about the food. With this new way of living, mindset is essential.

Measurement conversion

The following table provides a comparison chart for cooking your dishes using both imperial and metric units of measurement. Are you looking for a basic baking diagram or metric and imperial kitchen cooking calculations?

A necessary kitchen tool is a measuring conversion chart. Enjoy this simple to use conversion chart for cooking, which includes measurements for a number of dry and liquid conversions.

Ever desired a recipe in half? Your measuring cup is broken, and you need to measure out 1/4 cup of flour. Although numerous alternative measurements have been employed and unit definitions have changed, the "International System of Units," or current iteration of the metric method, is still utilized as the majority of nations' official measurement system.

Conversion Units Chart

A few grains (dry)	=	Less than 1/8 teaspoon
3 tsp	=	1 tsp
1/2 tsp	=	1-1/2 tsp
1 tsp	=	3 tsp
2 tsp	=	1 fluid ounce
4 tsp	=	1/4 cup
5-1/3 tsp	=	1/3 cup
8 tsp	=	1/2 cup
8 tsp	=	4 fluid ounces

10-2/3 tsp	=	2/3 cup
12 tsp	=	3/4 cup
16 tsp	=	1 cup
6 tsp	=	8 fluid ounces
1/8 cup	=	2 tsp
1/4 cup	=	4 tsp
1/2 cup	=	8 tsp
1 cup	=	16 tablespoons
1 cup	=	8 fluid ounces
1 cup	=	1/2 pint
2 cups	=	1 pint
2 pints	=	1 quart
4 quarts (liquid)	=	1 gallon
8 quarts (dry)	=	1 peck
4 pecks (dry)	=	1 bushel
1 kg	=	about 2 pounds
1 lit	=	about 4 cups or 1 quart

Chapter 2

Breakfast Recipes

The Mediterranean diet is simple to follow for lunch or dinner. However, don't skip breakfast! The Mediterranean diet's guiding principles apply the same in the morning as they do at any other time: choose whole, healthy meals, such as plenty of fruits and vegetables, and avoid highly processed foods or saturated fats.

Use healthy olive oil as a cooking fat or to sprinkle on foods like morning scrambles, whole-wheat toast, and more whenever possible. Where you can, focus on eating lots of wholesome seasonal veggies, and have some sliced fruit as a side or snack. Here is what the Mediterranean diet suggests you eat for breakfast.

1. Bowl of Blueberry Smoothie

Fresh fruits, flaxseed seeds, butter, and other ingredients are combined in this blueberry smoothie to give your morning bowl a boost of protein, good fats, nutrients, and fibre. It can be consumed as a bowl or as a beverage.

Ingredients

- Frozen blueberries, one cup
- Unsweetened almond milk in a half-cup
- Protein powder, 1 1/2 scoops
- Unsweetened almond butter, 2 tablespoons
- Pure vanilla extract, 1 teaspoon
- Fresh blueberries, half a cup
- Vanilla granola, 1/4 cup
- sliced almonds, 2 tablespoons
- 2 teaspoons hemp seeds
- Ground cinnamon, 1 teaspoon

Directions

- Using a blender, thoroughly combine the almond milk, protein powder, almond butter, and vanilla extract until completely smooth. Distribute across two bowls.
- Before serving, garnish each bowl with fresh blueberries, granola, hazelnuts, hemp seeds, and cinnamon.

2. Slow Cooker Mediterranean Frittata

What can you cook for breakfast that looks incredibly elegant but requires almost little work? Why, this Mediterranean frittata cooked slowly. Basically, you just dump all the ingredients into your Crock-Pot and get on with your day while it cooks. Every morning ought to be this simple (and delicious).

Ingredients

- 8 eggs
- milk, 1/3 cup
- Oregano, dry, 1 teaspoon
- Add salt and pepper (black)
- Arugula infant, 4 cups
- 1 1/4 cups chopped red peppers, roasted
- 12 cups of red onion, finely sliced
- 1/4 cup goat cheese crumbles

Directions

- Spray nonstick cooking spray inside the slow cooker.
- Combine the eggs, milk, and oregano in a big basin by whisking them together. To taste, add salt and pepper to the food.
- Put the baby arugula, goat cheese, red onion, and roasted red peppers in the slow cooker. Over the vegetables, pour the eggs.
- Cook for 2 12 to 3 hours on low. Serve right away.

3. Cranberry Walnut Grain-Free Granola

Pristine store-bought granola had better be on the lookout. This grain-free variation is tastier and healthier than the sugar cereal that passes for hippy food because it is made with a variety of seeds and nuts.

Ingredients

- 2 cups roughly chopped walnuts
- half a cup of dried cherries or cranberries
- Pumpkin seeds, 1/4 cup
- Sunflower seeds, 3 tablespoons
- three tablespoons of flaxseeds or hemp seeds
- 3 teaspoons of melted olive oil or coconut oil
- 2 teaspoons of maple syrup, pure.
- 1 tablespoon of vanilla extract purified
- 1 tablespoon cinnamon powder
- Pumpkin pie spice, 2 teaspoons
- sea salt, one teaspoon

Directions

- Prepare a baking sheet by lining it with parchment paper, and then preheat the oven to 150 degrees Celsius (300 degrees Fahrenheit). Put all of the ingredients into a bowl of medium size and mix them together thoroughly so that the mixture covers everything.
- Spread the mixture onto the prepared baking sheet, and bake for 15 to 17 minutes, stirring occasionally, until golden brown.

4. Poached Eggs Caprese

With mozzarella, tomato, and pesto, these Caprese eggs are a delectable dish that was inspired by eggs Benedict.

Ingredients

- 1 tablespoon of white vinegar, distilled
- two salty teaspoons
- 4 eggs
- 2 split English muffins
- 4 slices (1 ounce) mozzarella cheese
- 1 tomato, cut thickly
- Pesto, 4 tablespoons
- salt as desired

Directions

- 2 to 3 inches of water should be added to a big pot, and it should be heated to a rolling boil. Add vinegar and two tablespoons of salt lower the heat to medium-low, and maintain a moderate simmer in the water.
- While waiting for the water to simmer, top each English muffin half with a single slice of tomato and a piece of mozzarella cheese. Toast the English muffins in a slow cooker for about five minutes, or until the muffins have a golden color. until the English muffin is golden.
- The egg is cracked into a little basin. Gently lower the egg into simmering water while maintaining the bowl just above the water's surface. Continue with the remaining eggs. Eggs should be poached for 2 1/2 to 3 minutes, or until the whites are solid and the yolks are thick but still soft. Take the eggs out of the water using something like a slotted spoon, and wipe them dry with a dish towel to eliminate any further moisture.
- On top of each egg, sprinkle it with salt to taste then add a teaspoon of pesto sauce.

5. Egg and Veggie Breakfast Bowl

Whatever you choose to eat it with—a salad for breakfast or eggs for dinner—this bowl of vegetables and protein will keep you full for a long time.

Ingredients

- Brussels sprouts, 1 pound
- 100 grams of sweet potatoes
- Olive oil, 1 1/2 tablespoons
- Arugula, two cups
- 4 eggs
- Harissa, 2 tablespoons
- apple cider vinegar, 3 teaspoons

Directions

- Adjust the temperature in the oven to 400 degrees Fahrenheit. Cover a parchment paper-covered baking sheet to prevent it from getting dirty. Halve the Brussels sprouts. The sweet potatoes into dice.
- On the baking sheet, arrange the yams and Brussels sprouts in a single layer. The vegetables should be seasoned with salt and pepper, and olive oil should be drizzled over them equally.
- To get the desired golden brown color and tenderness, roast the vegetables from 17 to 20 minutes. Combine the harissa, olive oil, and apple cider vinegar in a small bowl.
- Fry or poach the eggs.
- To assemble the dishes, divide the Brussels sprouts and sweet potatoes among the four bowls. Add 1 egg and 1/2 cup of arugula to each bowl. Add two teaspoons of the harissa vinaigrette to each bowl.

6. Sweet Potato Rösti with Fried Eggs

Similar to latkes or potato pancakes, rösti are a Swiss dish. For added flavor, color, and nutrition, sweet potatoes are used in the preparation of these. (I need to buy some beta carotene.)

Ingredients

- 1 pound of shredded and peeled sweet potatoes
- 1 substantial shallot, minced
- Brown rice flour, 2 teaspoons
- 2 tablespoons of fresh cilantro, chopped finely.
- Lightly beaten, one large egg
- 1/2 kosher salt spoon
- 12 tsp of cumin seeds
- Freshly ground black pepper, a pinch
- Use olive oil while cooking
- Four big eggs, to be fried
- To serve, arugula

Directions

- Combine the cilantro, sweet potato, shallot, brown rice flour, egg, salt, cumin, and pepper in a big bowl.
- Add enough olive oil to a big skillet to cover the bottom while it's heating up over medium heat. Scoop approximately a quarter cup of the sweet potato mixture onto the skillet, flatten it, and cook for about three minutes on each side until crispy (be careful not to burn it). Once you have 12 rösti altogether, continue with the remaining sweet potato mixture and transfer the remaining rösti to a plate coated with paper towels using a spatula.
- Put two eggs with their shells in the pan, season them with salt and pepper, and let them fry for about five minutes, or until the whites are set as well as the edges are crispy. Fry the remaining 2 eggs after removing the already fried ones from the pan. Top the rösti with fried eggs and arugula before serving.

7. Pan Con Tomato (Spain)

The pan con tomato that we prepare here in Guadalajara, Spain, and that is served in pubs and eateries throughout Spain, is based on a long-standing Catalan custom. The Catalan practice, formerly known as "pa amb tomaquet," involved taking stale bread and rubbing it with raw garlic and tomato slices before drizzling it with olive oil and lightly salting it.

Ingredients

- Cut a half baguette into 1-inch rounds.
- one garlic clove
- 1 medium-sized ripe tomato
- Extra virgin olive oil, two tablespoons
- a dash of salt

Directions

- To remove the skin from the garlic, use a knife to crush the skin. Half a tomato that is ripe. To a blender, add the garlic, tomato, 2 Tablespoons of olive oil, and a dash of salt. Until smooth, puree.
- In a toaster oven or oven set to broil, toast baguette slices.
- Each piece of bread should have a thin layer of olive oil and a teaspoon of tomato sauce on top.
- Add Prosciutto, Jamon Iberico, Jamon Serrano, tuna, or salmon on top.

8. Spinach and Goat Cheese Quiche

Try this veggie French quiche for breakfast. For a novel Mediterranean treat, spinach & goat cheese take the place of ham and shredded cheese.

Ingredients

- 1 pie crust, frozen
- 3 eggs
- half a cup of half and half
- 3 tablespoons of sour cream
- spinach, fresh, 10 ounces
- 6 delicious goat cheese slices (around 2 ounces)
- 1/2 teaspoon salt
- Black pepper, 1/4 teaspoon

Directions

- While you prepare the remaining ingredients, take the crust out of the freezer and allow it to thaw.
- Oven temperature set to 390 °F.
- Slice the spinach finely. In a skillet, cook them with up to 1/4 cup water. Cook spinach just till it wilts. Squeeze the spinach to remove any remaining moisture after draining the water.
- Whisk the eggs in a medium bowl before adding the half & half, sour cream, salt, and pepper. until smooth, whisk. With a spoon or spatula, add the spinach and combine.
- Fill the pie crust with egg mixture. Add slices of goat cheese on top.
- Bake the quiche for about 45 minutes, or until it has set.

9. Traditional Italian Biscotti

Make your own homemade almond biscotti (cantucci), a classic Italian delicacy that is baked twice. Organize in 15 minutes, then bake for 30. The Mediterranean is very simple!

Ingredients

- Unpeeled almonds in a cup
- Sugar, 1 1/4 cups
- Three eggs plus one for brushing.
- 1 tablespoon of honey
- 3 cups regular flour
- Baking powder, 1 teaspoon
- one orange rind
- 1 dash of salt

Directions

- Set oven to 370 degrees.
- Chop the almonds, half of them, roughly.
- Combine sugar, honey, and eggs in a sizable bowl. The combination will become lighter in color after you whisk it for a few minutes.
- Salt, baking soda, orange zest, and flour should be added. All of the ingredients should be thoroughly mixed.
- The almonds—both chopped and whole—should be added once the mixture has a crumbly consistency. Place the three long logs of dough (each about 1 1/2 inches high) on a baking sheet that has been lined with parchment paper. Don't forget to leave enough room between the logs so they can rise.
- Apply egg evenly to the log's surface.
- Until golden brown, bake for 20 minutes.
- Take the logs out of the oven and turn the temperature down the temperature to 165 C. Use a knife with a serrated edge to cut diagonal slices of half an inch thickness from the logs.
- Place the cut sides of the slices down on the baking sheet once more. Cook for an additional 8–10 minutes.

10. Shakshuka

In a simmering tomato sauce with spices, poached eggs are the main component of the North African and Middle Eastern dish shakshuka. It is quick to prepare, healthful, and only needs a few minutes. See how quickly it comes together in the above video!

Ingredients

- Olive oil, two tablespoons
- diced one medium onion
- 1 chopped and seeded red bell pepper
- 4 garlic cloves, chopped finely
- paprika, 2 teaspoons
- 1/9 cup cumin
- 1 bunch of chopped parsley
- 1/4 tsp. chili powder
- 1 bunch of fresh cilantro, chopped
- 1 entire, peeled 28-ounce can of tomatoes
- 6 eggs
- add salt and pepper to taste

Directions

- On medium heat, warm the olive oil in a sizable sauté pan. When the onion is transparent, add the diced red pepper and onion and cook for an additional 5 minutes. After combining the garlic and spices, cook for an additional minute. Use a large spoon to break up the tomatoes as you pour the tomato juice and tomatoes from the can into the pan. Braising the sauce while adding salt and pepper as needed.
- Create small wells in the sauce with your large spoon, and then crack an egg into each well. Cook the eggs for 5-10 min, or until they're done to your liking, under cover. Add chopped parsley and cilantro as a garnish.

11. Mediterranean Tostadas

The ideal recipe for an easy lunch or dinner is these vegan Mediterranean tostadas! They are flavorful and easy to prepare in only 10 minutes.

Ingredients

For salad

- green olives, chopped, half a cup
- 1 1/2 cups of chopped cucumbers
- 1/4 cup diced red onion or shallot
- 14 cups finely minced parsley
- 1 cup of chopped cherry tomatoes
- Olive oil, 1 tbsp
- Juice from a half-lemon
- Pepper and salt to taste

For the tostadas

- 6 tortillas, I like corn
- 1/2 cup Mediterranean salad with hummus
- Tahini*

Directions

- Get the salad ready. In a mixing dish, combine the cucumbers, tomatoes, olives, shallots, and parsley. Mix the ingredients for the dressing in a separate bowl, then pour it over the salad. Combine by tossing.
- Construct the tostadas. Corn tortillas should be crisp and golden when being toasted. I put around 2 teaspoons of hummus on top, followed by 1/4 cup of the salad. Enjoy after adding tahini drizzle!

12. Mediterranean Sandwich

A quick and spicy vegetarian Mediterranean sandwich! Fresh basil pesto, a tonne of vegetables, and creamy feta cheese are spread across hearty bread. Although this recipe is for one sandwich, you may scale it to make however many you'd like!

Ingredients

- 2 slices of robust bread
- A couple of teaspoons of fresh basil pesto
- 1 teaspoon of real mayonnaise
- One-half teaspoon of Sriracha sauce
- 1/4 cup of baby spinach, lightly packed
- 10 strips of red onion, very thinly sliced
- 3 to 4 teaspoons of feta cheese crumbles
- 4 Campari tomato slices
- Add some sea salt and black pepper on top.
- 6 strips of well-drained, jarred roasted red pepper

Directions

- Put two slices of bread on the table. One slice should have pesto on one side. Mayo and Sriracha should be mixed together in a small bowl (add slowly and to heat preference). On the other piece of bread, spread this mayo on one side.
- To adhere the baby spinach to the mayo and Sriracha, lightly push down on top of it. Gently press the red onion pieces, which have been finely cut, onto the pesto-covered side. On top of the red onion, sprinkle the feta cheese, and then gently press it in place. Don't skimp because this will melt down a little bit? The finely diced tomatoes are added after a small amount of salt and black pepper is sprinkled on top. The red pepper strips that have been well drained. Put the spinach-topped sandwich piece on top of the other.
- Sandwich added to an electric grill or panini press. You could also add it to a dry skillet. For an electric grill, close the lid and cook for 3 to 5 minutes, or until the cheese is melted

and the bread is thoroughly toasted with visible char marks. For a panini press: Place the sandwich in and cook for 3 to 5 minutes, or as directed by the maker, until golden and the cheese is melted.

- In a frying pan: A dry skillet should be heated to medium-low. Place the sandwich on top, and then place a pan on top to add weight. After flipping, cook for an extra 2 to 3 minutes.

13. Egg muffins

Easy and nutritious egg muffins for breakfast these freezer-friendly, low-crab egg muffins are a fantastic option for breakfast on the road. Serve alongside salad and other Mediterranean favorites for your upcoming brunch as well; read the notes for suggestions!

Ingredients

- Olive oil extra virgin for brushing
- 1 small red bell pepper, almost 3/4 cup, chopped
- One shallot, chopped finely, six to ten pitted kalamata olives, chopped, and one ounce (28.34 grams, or approximately 12 cups) of cooked, boneless chicken or turkey. fresh parsley leaves, chopped

- To your liking, add a handful of feta crumbles.
- 8 large eggs
- Pepper and salt
- Spanish paprika, 1/2 tsp.
- 1/4 teaspoon ground turmeric (optional)

Directions

- With a rack in the centre, your oven must be preheated at 350 degrees Fahrenheit.
- Prepare a 12-cup muffin pan, like this one, or 12 separate muffin cups. Brush with extra virgin olive oil. Divide the chicken (or turkey), peppers, tomatoes, shallots, olives, parsley, and crushed feta among the 12 cups; fill each one to about two-thirds full.

- Add the eggs, salt, peppers, and spices to a sizable measuring cup or mixing bowl. To blend, whisk thoroughly.

- Carefully pour the egg mixture into each cup; leaving a small space at the top (should be approximately 3/4 of the way up).

- To assist catch any spillage, place a sheet pan on atop of a cupcake pan or muffin cups. Bake the egg muffins in a pre - heated oven for around 30 min, or until they have set.

- After a few minutes of cooling, loosen each muffin's edges by running a small butter knife around their perimeters. Serve after removing from pan!

14. Mediterranean Breakfast Quesadilla

Mediterranean Breakfast Quesadilla: Prepared in only 10 minutes, this simple, delicious breakfast dish features eggs, cheese, and vegetables.

Ingredients

- 2 cooked and scrambled eggs
- quarter cup mozzarella
- Slices of basil, a tomato, and a pinch of salt and pepper, to taste
- one tortilla

Directions

- Don't overcook the eggs when scrambling them. To taste, add salt and pepper.

- Lay the eggs across half of a tortilla.

- Add basil, tomato slices, and mozzarella cheese on top.

- The tortilla is folded, and then it is toasted till golden brown on both sides on an oiled pan.

- Slice and serve right away, or consume while on the go.

15. Breakfast Tacos

These straightforward, healthful breakfast tacos are stuffed with eggs, herbs, and fresh vegetables.

Ingredients

- 2 tiny corn or wheat tortillas
- 1 teaspoon olive oil and two eggs
- 1 cup spinach, halved cherry tomatoes, and 1/2 cup
- 2 teaspoons crumbled feta
- 1 tablespoon of freshly chopped basil,
- Add salt and pepper to taste

Directions

- On medium heat, warm the olive oil in the pan. In a bowl, whisk the eggs before adding them, to the hot pan. When they are cooked to your taste, stir occasionally. To taste, add salt and pepper.
- Tortillas with spinach should have scrambled eggs on top. The feta, basil, and tomatoes.

Chapter 3

Rice, Grains and Pasta Recipes

A grain that is rich in nutrients is brown rice. It still has the germ and bran in contrast to even more processed white rice. In addition to being healthier than white rice, brown rice has a nuttier, more nuanced flavor, which makes it the ideal foundation for bowls, salads, and casseroles. These few ideas for healthy brown rice include sides, entrees, and desserts. If you don't frequently prepare recipes with brown rice, this is the perfect time to start because the grain is adaptable, healthy, and simple to prepare.

1. Tuscan Mediterranean Brown Rice

My nutritious and filling Mediterranean bowl it's the ideal one bowl supper because it's loaded with brown rice, tahini, and roasted tomatoes.

Ingredients

- Olive oil aerosol
- 1 can (15 oz) drained garbanzo beans
- 1/2-inch chunks of one medium zucchini, sea salt, and pepper.
- Sun-dried tomato olive oil, two tablespoons
- 3 minced garlic cloves
- 1 chopped medium white onion
- 4 cups brown rice, medium-grain, cooked
- 1/3 cup tightly packed chopped parsley
- 1/2 cup chopped sun-dried tomatoes and 1/2 cup chopped fresh dill
- sliced or diced Kalamata olives, 4 ounces
- Two tablespoons. The seasoning from Fit Cook Land
- 1 tablespoon lemon zest, 1 tablespoon lemon juice, sea salt, and freshly ground pepper

Directions

- On high, heat a skillet. Once hot, drizzle with a little olive oil, and then add the zucchini and garbanzo beans. They should have dark sear marks on them after 1 to 2 minutes of resting in the skillet without moving. After another minute of cooking, mix and take out of the skillet.

- Pour the tomato oil, garlic, and onions into the skillet once it has cooled to medium heat. The onions should be cooked for about three to five minutes, or until they are slightly transparent and golden.

- Add the (cooled) brown rice, black bean mixture, onions, and the remaining ingredients to a sizable mixing bowl. Mix well, then season with sea pepper and salt as desired.

2. Tomato Brown Rice Pilaf

Brown rice, fresh tomatoes, and hearty Mediterranean spices are used to make this tomato rice. It's the perfect side dish, and I'll demonstrate to you how to cook it!

Ingredients

- Olive oil, two tablespoons
- 1 yellow onion, chopped finely
- 3 minced cloves of garlic
- 2 cups of long-grain brown rice
- One cumin teaspoon
- Cinnamon, 1/2 teaspoon
- A quarter cup of tomato paste
- 2 seeded and finely chopped Roma tomatoes
- 1 salt teaspoon
- 3 cups of vegetable broth low in sodium
- For garnish, use 1/4 cup fresh cilantro leaves.

Directions

- To release as much starch as possible, agitate the rice with your hands as you rinse it in cold water until the water runs clear. Place the rice in a mesh sieve. Place aside.

- Medium heat is used to warm the oil in a large saucepan. Add the onions and simmer for a further 2-3 minutes, stirring occasionally, until soft. One minute later, add the garlic and cook it until fragrant. Cook for an additional two minutes, stirring in the rinsed rice, tomato paste, cumin, cinnamon, chopped tomatoes, and salt.
- Add the veggie stock once the mixture has to a boil. Once the liquid has been absorbed and the rice is tender, turn down the heat, cover the pan, and simmer for 45 minutes.
- Remove from heat, cover the rice, and let it steam for an additional five minutes. With a fork, uncover and fluff. Add some fresh cilantro before serving.

3. Mediterranean Yellow Rice

Rice made with this quick and simple Mediterranean yellow rice recipe is the fluffiest and tastiest! Serve this vegetarian Greek pilaf alongside grilled veggies, lamb koftas, or kebobs. Toasted pine nuts can be added for crunch.

Ingredients

- 2 tablespoons of olive or avocado oil
- 12 of a finely chopped sweet onion
- smashed three garlic cloves
- 34 teaspoon turmeric
- 1/4 tsp. cumin
- 1/4 tsp. paprika
- To taste, 1 14 tsp. salt
- 1 1/2 cups of drained and washed basmati rice
- 1.5 cups of water
- 1/4 cup of crunchy pine nuts
- 2 tablespoons chopped finely, cilantro
- 2 teaspoons of finely chopped flat-leaf parsley

Directions

- In a medium-sized pot on a medium-high heat, add oil & onion dice. Sauté onion for two to three minutes, or until transparent. After adding the garlic, continue to simmer for one more minute. Add salt, paprika, cumin, and turmeric. Till fragrant, toast. (Roughly one minute.)

- Rice is next added after adding water and scraping any sticky food from the bottom of the saucepan. After properly combining all of the ingredients, bring the water to a boil.
- When the pot is boiling, put a lid on it and lower the heat. 20 minutes of simmering is required to achieve fluffy and soft rice. Add the chopped cilantro, parsley, and toasted pine nuts after turning off the heat in the pot. Serve right away!

4. Mediterranean Chicken and Rice

Mediterranean Chicken with Rice is simple, flavorful, and absolutely delicious. made with precisely cooked yellow jasmine rice and chicken thighs. It is a go-to recipe for midweek meals!

Ingredients

For the chicken:

- 5 thighs deboned
- 1.5 teaspoons of dried oregano
- 1 teaspoon of dried parsley
- 1tsp paprika
- 1 tsp salt
- Juice from one lemon, 1/4 cup
- half tsp pepper
- 1-tablespoon olive oil

Regarding the yellow rice:

- 1 cup white rice, either Basmati or Jasmine.
- 2 cups low-sodium chicken broth
- 2 tablespoons unsalted butter
- 1/2 cup sliced white onions (yellow onions are also acceptable!
- 4 minced garlic cloves
- 1/2 teaspoon of turmeric
- 0.5 teaspoon cumin
- One cinnamon stick
- garnish with fresh parsley

Directions

- Set the oven to 350° F. Chicken thighs should be combined with oregano, parsley, and paprika, lemon juice, salt, and pepper in a medium bowl.

- Medium heat should be applied to a cast iron skillet. When the oil is hot, add the chicken and cook it for about 3 to 4 minutes on each side in the cast iron skillet (or other pan) that you are using. Even if the chicken doesn't finish cooking, it will still be cooked thoroughly in the oven.

- The chicken should be taken out of the cast iron and placed on a plate. While maintaining the castings on medium high heat, melt the butter and add the diced onion. After cooking for two to three minutes, add garlic and stir.

- After that, stir for 30 seconds while adding the uncooked rice. Stir in the cinnamon, cumin, turmeric, and chicken broth. After removing the skillet from the heat, throw the chicken back in on topping of the uncooked rice.

- When the rice is cooked and the chicken reaches an internal temperature of 165° F, cover it with foil and bake in the preheated oven for 35–40 minutes. Rice should be tasted before seasoning, and as needed, more salt or pepper can be added. Enjoy adding parsley and other garnishes of your choice!

5. Greek lemon rice

Best recipe for Greek lemon rice! Fresh herbs, lemon juice, onions, and garlic provide tons of flavors. For suggestions and advice on what to accompany it with, refer to the notes.

Ingredients

- two cups of long-grained rice (uncooked)
- Greek extra virgin olive oil from the early harvest
- 1 minced garlic clove
- 1/2 cup of orzo pasta
- 1 cup of onions, chopped
- lemon juice from two (PLUS zest of 1 lemon)
- Salt, a pinch
- 2 cups of salt-free broth

- A large amount of freshly chopped parsley
- 1 teaspoon dill weed (dry dill)

Directions

- You ought to be able to shatter a grain of rice easily by simply placing it between your index and thumb and doing so repeatedly.
- Approximately three tablespoons of extra virgin olive oil should be heated in a large sauce pan that has a lid, such as this one, until the oil shimmers but does not smoke. When translucent, add the onions and simmer for a further 3 to 4 minutes. Orzo pasta and garlic are added. Stir in the rice after a brief tossing period, once the orzo has begun to take on some color Coat by tossing.
- Now add the broth, as well as the lemon juice. After heating the liquid to a rolling boil, reduce the heat to a low setting. Cover the pot and continue to cook the rice for another 15 to 20 minutes, during which time the liquid should have been completely absorbed, and the rice should be soft but not sticky.
- Take the rice off the heat. For optimal results, cover the rice and don't touch it for roughly ten minutes. Parsley, dill, and lemon zest are added after removing the cover. Add some lemon slices as a garnish if you'd like. Enjoy!

6. Mediterranean grain bowl

These crisp, flavorful, full grain bowls from the Mediterranean region are vegetarian and delightful. Make your bowl unique and prepare the food. Your favorite cereals, vegetables, greens, and proteins can all be included. A savory lemon tahini herb dressing can then be drizzled over everything.

Ingredients

For the bowl

- two cups of spinach
- One cup of arugula
- 1/3 cup ready Couscous
- roasted potatoes in a cup
- 3 balls of lentils
- Black olives, five
- half a cup of crunchy chickpeas

- 3 teaspoons of oil-braised artichoke hearts
- 1/0 cup red onions that have been pickled
- Cut cucumbers

As a dressing

- ½ cup of tahini
- 1/4 cup of Greek yogurt, plain
- One teaspoon of lemon juice
- two fresh thyme leaf sprigs
- fresh rosemary leaves, half a sprig
- 3 roasted garlic cloves
- Cold water, 1/2 cup (more or less, as needed)

Directions

- Preparing the potatoes: Potatoes that have been peeled and cubed are tossed in with oil and a tablespoon of dijon mustard. Season to taste with salt and pepper. Keep baking at 400 degrees Fahrenheit (200 degrees Celsius) for another 35 to 45 minutes or until meat is easily pierced with a fork.
- To cook the couscous, add olive oil to taste, and then transfer half a cup into a bowl. Add a lid after stirring with a fork after adding 1 cup of boiling water. After 5 minutes, give it a little stir with a fork.
- Planting the seeds for chickpeas In a large skillet, heat the oil over medium heat. Season with salt and pepper and mix in the chickpeas. Cook, tossing, until crispy, approximately 10 minutes.
- To make the dressing, mix all of the ingredients (apart from the water) in a small food processor or blender, and blend until thoroughly incorporated. As needed, add water to thin it down. Tahini and water will first clash, causing the mixture to thicken up; this is natural and okay; simply keep adding water until the mixture emulsifies and thins to your preference.
- Prepare by warming your preferred vegetable balls and slicing cucumber.
- Build the bowl: Include the greens, lentil balls, 1/3 cup couscous, 1/3 cup potatoes, 1/3 cup crispy chickpeas, 1/3 cup cucumber, 1/3 cup artichokes, 1/3 cup olives, and 1/3 cup pickled red onions. Add the dressing and then serve.

7. Almond Joy Granola

With maple syrup, this healthy granola recipe is naturally sweet (or honey). It contains coconut oil, your preferred nuts and fruits, as well as oats. Adapt it to suit you! 8 cups of granola, or roughly 16 half-cup servings, are produced by the recipe.

Ingredients

- Old-fashioned rolled oats, 4 cups
- 1 1/2 cups raw seeds and/or nuts
- 1 teaspoon of sea salt, fine-grained
- ½ teaspoon of cinnamon powder
- heated coconut oil or olive oil, 1/2 cup
- ½ cup honey or maple syrup
- Vanilla extract, 1 teaspoon
- 2/3 cup chopped dried fruit, if large
- Add-ins is entirely optional, such as 1/2 cup of chocolate chips or coconut flakes.

Directions

- Prepare an extra-large baking sheet with a rim and turn the oven temperature up to 350 degrees Fahrenheit. In a large mixing bowl, combine the oats, the nuts and/or seeds, the salt, and the cinnamon. To combine, stir.

- Add the vanilla, honey, and/or maple syrup to the oil. Mix thoroughly until each nut and grain is just lightly coated. On the baking sheet that has been prepared, use a large spoon to spread the granola so that it forms a uniform layer.
- After baking for 21 to 24 minutes, at which time you should stir the granola halfway through the process if you want it to be extra clumpy, push the stirred granola firmly with your spoon to form a more even layer. The crunchiness of the granola will increase as it is allowed to cool.

- Untouched, let the granola cools fully (at least 45 minutes). Add the dried fruit on top (and optional chocolate chips, if using). If you want to keep the granola in large chunks, break it into bits with your hands; if you don't want it to be overly clumpy, stir it using a spoon.

- For one to two weeks at room temperature, or for up to three months in the freezer, store the granola in an airtight container. Before serving, allow the dried fruit to return to room temp for five to ten minutes, as it is prone to solidifying when frozen.

8. Four- ingredients granola

This five-minute gluten-free granola recipe just calls for four vegan ingredients. The top GF granola has crunchy clusters, nutritious ingredients, and a delicious flavor!

Ingredients

- 1 ½ cups of roughly chopped nuts (almonds, pecans, walnuts, etc.)
- 1 cup rolled oats without gluten
- ½ cup blanched, finely ground almond flour
- ½ teaspoon of cinnamon powder (optional)
- 4 grains of salt (optional)
- 4 ounces of pure maple syrup

Directions

- The oven should be heated to 325°F. Use oiled foil or parchment paper to line a sizable baking sheet. Put it off till later.

- Everything should be put in a big bowl. Use a rubber spatula to fold the ingredients until clusters form, at which point they are considered completely incorporated.

- Pour on the baking sheet you have prepared. Spread the granola out evenly with the spatula. To make clusters, separate the granola into little mounds. Make room between the clusters so that air may pass through and cause the granola to become crisp.

- For 20 minutes, bake. Flip the granola using a heat-resistant spatula, being careful to preserve the clusters. Continue baking the granola for an additional five to fifteen mins, or until the rims are a rich golden brown color. Mine took 30 minutes in total. Granola will become crispier as it cools.

- Position cooling rack over the baking sheet. Allow it to cool entirely, or for around 30 minutes. Enjoy!

9. Mediterranean Lentil and Grain Bowls

These Mediterranean Lentil and Grain Bowls are delicious but simple to prepare, full of fibre and protein, and perfect for weekday meals as well as meal prepping.

Ingredients

For pickled onions

- a single medium red onion
- 180 mL or 3/4 cup of water
- 1 tsp maple syrup
- 1 1/2 teaspoons of sea salt, fine
- Half a cup of white vinegar
- Red pepper flakes, 1/4 to 1/2 teaspoon (optional)
- Peppercorns, whole, 1/2 teaspoon (optional)

For cooked lentils

- 1-teaspoons of olive oil
- One tablespoon of cumin seeds
- 6 minced garlic cloves
- 234 cups (640-660 mL) of vegetable broth
- 180g or 1 cup of French green lentils
- Sea salt or Kosher salt, as desired
- To taste, freshly cracked black pepper
- tahini, 2 tablespoons
- 2 to 3 tablespoons of tamari (depends on how salty your vegetable broth is)

For cooked farro

- Water 2 cups
- 1 cup of pearled farro
- Sea salt or Kosher salt
- 1 bay leaf (optional, for seasoning)
- fresh black pepper, freshly cracked (optional, for seasoning)
- 2 half-sliced garlic cloves (optional, for seasoning)

For hummus

- 1 can of chickpeas (15 ounces/440 grams) or 1 3/4 cups (260–280 grams) of cooked chickpeas
- 75g or 1/3 cup of tahini
- Juiced, 1 medium lemon (about 3 tablespoons)
- 2 chopped garlic cloves
- one to two teaspoons of ground cumin
- To taste, freshly cracked black pepper
- 1 tsp kosher salt
- four to six tablespoons of ice water

Directions

Directions for Pickled Onions

- Using a kettle or a burner, gently bring the water to a boil. The onion should be thinly cut. The onion pieces should be put in a big mason jar.
- Combine the peppercorns, salt, vinegar, maple syrup, boiling water, and red pepper flakes. Once the syrup or sugar has dissolved, stir to mix. Over the cut onions in the container, pour the pickling solution.
- Give the dish at least 30 minutes to cool to room temperature. You can serve them right away, but I like to chill them first to let the taste develop.
- Directions for Creamy Mediterranean Lentils
- The olive oil is added to a big, deep nonstick frying pan or Dutch oven that is already heated over medium heat. Once hot, add the cumin and garlic seeds and simmer, stirring regularly, for 1-2 minutes, or until fragrant.
- After deglazing the pan with the vegetable broth, add the lentils. The mixture should be brought to a boil, then quickly simmered for 25 to 30 minutes, or until the legumes are

tender but still have some bite.

- Incorporate the tahini and tamari thoroughly into the lentils before lowering the heat. Upon tasting the food, add salt and freshly cracked black pepper as desired.

Directions for Farro

- Bring the water to a boil in a small saucepan after adding the salt. Farro should be added together with the seasonings, simmered until al dente (tender but chewy), and then served. For pearled farro, it should require 15-20 minutes, and for semi-pearled farro, it should take 20–30 minutes.

- Drain the farro through a strainer once it is al dente, then throw away the aromatics. If you have the time, spread the farro out on a sheet tray to cool and dry out; this prevents it from turning mushy.

- The chickpeas should be added to a food processor and blended for 2 minutes, scraping down the sides as necessary with a silicone spatula, to create a thick paste-like purée.

- The tahini, lemon juice, cumin, garlic, and 1 teaspoon of salt should be added. As the machine is running, slowly stream in the ice water until the hummus is thick but creamy and smooth. If necessary, add additional cumin, lemon juice, or salt after tasting for seasoning. If the hummus is too thick, add more ice water.

- Cover the hummus with plastic wrap to avoid drying. 30 minutes should be ideal for resting before serving. When serving, sprinkle paprika, and basil over top.

10. One-Pot Tomato Basil Pasta

Simple, quick, and hassle-free midweek supper is this one-pot pasta dish with tangy tomato-basil sauce. You combine all of your ingredients in one pot, and after about 25 minutes of cooking and a little stirring, your family will have a nutritious meal.

Ingredients

- Whole-wheat rotini, 8 ounces
- one water cup
- 2 cups of chicken broth or low-sodium "no chicken" broth
- Olive oil, extra virgin, two tablespoons
- 15-ounce salt-free chopped tomatoes
- 1/2 teaspoon of salt
- Garlic powder, half a teaspoon
- Italian seasoning, 1 1/2 tablespoons
- onion powder, half a teaspoon
- 6 cups baby spinach or kale
- 1/2 cup of basil slices
- Red pepper flakes, 1/4 teaspoon
- garnished with grated Parmesan cheese

Directions

- In a big saucepan, mix pasta with water, broth, tomatoes, oil, Italian seasoning, onion, garlic, salt, and crushed red pepper. Cover and cook to a boil over high heat.
- Stirring continuously, remove the lid, and cook for ten minutes at medium-high heat.
- Add the kale and cook for another 5 to 7 minutes, stirring often, or until the majority of the fluid has been absorbed. Basil is mixed in. Adding Parmesan as a garnish is optional.

11. Chicken Parmesan Pasta

This chicken Parmigiano pasta uses the one-pot pasta approach to cook noodles, chicken, plus sauce in one skillet. For a lovely cheese crust, finish the dish under the broiler.

Ingredients

- Whole-wheat Panko breadcrumbs, 1/4 cup
- 1 tablespoon and 1 teaspoon of split minced garlic
- 1 teaspoon of seasoning mix
- 2 tbs olive oil
- 4 grains of salt
- 1 lb boneless breast
- 3 cups of chicken broth low in salt
- 1 1/2 cups of tomato-crushed
- Whole-wheat penne, 8 ounces
- Shredded mozzarella cheese in a half-cup
- 1/4 cup of grated Parmesan cheese
- 1/4 cup finely minced fresh basil

Directions

- 1 tablespoon oil in an oven-safe skillet over medium heat. Add 1 teaspoon of garlic and panko. For 1 to 2 minutes, stir-fry the panko until it turns golden brown. Place aside in a small basin after transfer. Clean the pan.
- Preheat 1 tablespoon oil in pan over medium heat. Add chicken, garlic, and salt.
- Cook for about 2 minutes, stirring regularly, or until the outside of the chicken is no longer pink. Tomatoes, broth, and penne are added. Bring to a boil and then cook, covered, stirring periodically, for fifteen to twenty minutes, until penne is prepared and the sauce has thickened. In the meantime, place an oven temperature in the upper third.
- The broiler should be set at high. Sprinkle mozzarella over the penne mixture when the pasta is finished cooking.

- Place the pan in the broiler and cook for about a minute, or until the mozzarella is bubbling and starting to brown. Add basil, Parmesan, and the panko mixture as a garnish.

12. Spinach, Chicken & Feta Pasta

This one-dish spaghetti recipe makes good use of Sunday meal preparation. Although the pasta is prepared in advance and kept in the refrigerator for use throughout the week, you can use any leftover cooked spaghetti you have on hand. This recipe tastes exceptionally wonderful with chicken sausage and feta.

Ingredients

- Olive oil, two tablespoons
- 3 cooked chicken sausage links, each weighing 9 ounces, cut into rounds.
- 1 cup of onion, chopped
- 5-ounce baby spinach
- 1 minced garlic clove
- 1 (8-ounce) can of tomato sauce with no salt added
- Cooked whole-wheat rotini pasta in six cups
- chopped, pitted Kalamata olives, 1/4 cup
- 12 cups of feta cheese, finely crumbled
- 14 cups finely minced fresh basil (Optional)

Directions

- Over medium-high heat, preheat the oil in a big straight-sided skillet. Simmer the sausage, onions, and garlic for four to six minutes, stirring often.
- Add pasta, tomato sauce, spinach, and olives. Cook, tossing frequently, for 3 to 5 minutes, or until the spaghetti is bubbling hot and the spinach is wilted.
- If additional water is required to prevent the spaghetti from sticking, add 1 to 2 tablespoons.

13. Chicken Pesto Pasta with Asparagus

Thanks to convenience supplies like rotisserie chicken and pre-made pesto, this nutritious chicken pesto pasta recipe is simple to create. Fresh asparagus enhances the flavor and appearance of this simple one-pot meal. If you have any on hand, fresh basil makes a great finishing touch.

Ingredients

- Whole-wheat penne, 8 ounces
- 1 pound of freshly cut, 2-inch-long spears of asparagus
- 3 cups cooked chicken breast shreds
- 1 (7-ounce) container of chilled pesto with basil
- 1 salt shaker-full
- 1/4 teaspoon of pepper, ground
- 1 ounce of grated Parmesan cheese (approximately 1/4 cup)
- fresh basil leaves, small for garnish

Directions

- Cook the pasta and Asparagus should be added to the pot during the last two minutes of cooking. Reserving 1/2 cup of cooking water, drain.
- Add the chicken, pesto, salt, and pepper to the spaghetti mixture before adding it back to the saucepan. To get the appropriate consistency, stir in the reserved cooking water, 1 tbsp. Top the dish with Parmesan and basil, if desired. Serve now.

14. Macaroni with Sausage & Ricotta

In this nutritious and speedy pasta dish, a little bit of sausage goes a long way in flavoring the creamy ricotta tomato sauce.

Ingredients

- Olive oil, extra virgin, two tablespoons
- 6 tablespoons of yellow onion, cut coarsely.
- 6 ounces of mild pork sausage with no casings
- 1 14-ounce can of chopped, whole, unsalted tomatoes with juice
- 14 teaspoons of pepper, ground
- 1 tablespoon plus 1/8 teaspoon of salt, divided
- 12 ounces of thin, tube-shaped pasta, like ceppo,
- Part-skim ricotta cheese, 6 teaspoons
- 10 finely sliced fresh basil leaves
- fresh Parmigianino Reggiano cheese, 1/4 cup

Directions

- In a large skillet, put the oil, onion, and sausage, and cook them over medium-high heat. Cook for 4 to 5 minutes, stirring and breaking up the sausage with a spoon, or until the onion is golden. Cook for 5 to 10 minutes, or until the tomatoes have reduced and separated from the oil, after adding the tomatoes, pepper, and 1/8 teaspoon salt. Get rid of the heat.
- Pasta should be cooked as directed on the package, in the boiling water with the remaining 1 tablespoon of salt.
- Return the sauce to medium-low heat just before the pasta is finished cooking. Stir in the ricotta and basil after adding them. After it has been properly drained, the pasta should be mixed with the sauce & Parmigianino before serving. Serve as soon as possible.

15. Halibut, Garlic, and Butter Spaghetti

This Halibut, Garlic, and Butter Spaghetti will be ready in less than 30 minutes. The delicate fish fillet that goes with this light pasta dish has been cooked with garlic, butter, parsley, chili, and olive oil. Lemon wedges should be placed on the side of the fish pasta dish. Just delicious!

Ingredients

- Halibut Fillets, about 1 ½ pounds, skin removed
- 4 tablespoons of crumbs
- 3 tablespoons of flat-leaf parsley, finely chopped
- 1 large lemon's zest
- 4 chopped garlic cloves
- 1 teaspoon chili flakes
- 1 tsp. sea salt
- Immediately Grinded Black Pepper
- Olive Oil, 6 Tbsp
- 2/TBS. Butter
- Twelve little Roma tomatoes
- 350-400 grams of dried spaghetti
- Citrus Wedges
- Parsley, Flat-Leaf, Finely Chopped

Directions

- Set the oven to 450 degrees.
- Breadcrumbs, fresh parsley, lemon zest, garlic, chili flakes, sea salt, and black pepper should all be combined in a small bowl.
- Two tablespoons of olive oil and aluminum foil are used to line and grease a sizable baking pan. The fish fillets should be placed on the baking tray, and then the tomato and breadcrumb mixture should be evenly distributed over them. Add butter on top and drizzle the remaining oil over the fish. Until the fish fillets are completely done, bake the fish for 12 to 13 minutes.
- While the fish is baking, prepare the noodles in accordance with the directions provided on the package. Once the pasta is al dente, drain it in a colander and combine it with the cooked fish. Add lemon juice, sea salt, black pepper, and some fresh parsley to taste.

Chapter 4

Poultry and Meats Recipes

Here, you'll learn how to add a touch of the Mediterranean to your home cooking, whether it's for a weeknight dinner or a special occasion dish. Below are some famous and easy to made poultry and meat recipes for you!

1. Greek sheet pan chicken

Greek sheet pan chicken is a complete dinner that features tender chicken thighs surrounded by colorful, caramelized veggies. You may have a fantastic dinner ready to go in just a few minutes by popping it in the oven!

Ingredients

- Olive oil, 1/2 cup
- Juiced lemon, one (about 3 tablespoons)
- 4 minced garlic cloves
- Oregano, 2 teaspoons dry
- one tablespoon of dried thyme
- Dijon mustard, 1 teaspoon
- 1 kosher salt tsp.
- freshly ground black pepper, half a teaspoon
- 6 skin-on, bone-in chicken thighs
- Sliced and half one medium zucchini.
- 1 yellow bell pepper, cut into pieces that are 1 inch long.
- 12 a large red onion, cut into wedges with a knife
- cherry or grape tomatoes, 1 pint
- 12 cup pitted kalamata olives
- 4 feta cheese cubes
- 2 tablespoons of fresh parsley, chopped finely.

Directions

- Preheat the oven to 425 degrees Fahrenheit. In a low-sided dish, combine the olive oil, lime juice, garlic, basil, thyme, and Dijon mustard. Season with salt and pepper.
- After putting the chicken thighs in a dish and pouring 2/3 of the marinade over them, you should use your hands to fully coat the chicken with the marinade so that it is evenly distributed. Whereas the chicken is marinating, spread the tomato, bell peppers, red onions, zucchini, and bell peppers out on a baking sheet & sprinkle the leftover marinade over the top. Combine all of the ingredients and toss to coat the vegetables. After placing the chicken thighs in the baking dish so that they are surrounded by the veggies, they need to be baked for another half an hour.
- After the chicken has reached an internal temperature of 165 degrees Fahrenheit and the veggies have reached the desired tenderness, remove the baking tray from the oven, sprinkle it with the olives, and then place it back in the oven for yet another 10 to 15 minutes.

2. Chicken kabobs

Greek chicken kabobs are deliciously flavorful and the ideal dish for grilling. Include a homemade tzaztiki sauce with this!

Ingredients

MARINADE

- Olive oil, 1/4 cup
- Red wine vinegar, 2 teaspoons
- Lemon juice, 3 teaspoons
- Dijon mustard, 1 teaspoon
- 3 minced garlic cloves
- Oregano, dry, 1 teaspoon
- 0.5 teaspoons of salt
- Black pepper, 1/4 teaspoon

BEEF KABOBS

- 3 boneless chicken in small chunks.
- Cut one red bell pepper into 1 1/2-inch chunk after seeding it.
- Cut one yellow bell pepper into 1 1/2-inch slice after seeding it.
- a single red onion, diced into 1 1/2-inch piece
- Sliced 1 zucchini

Directions

- To make the marinade, combine the canola oil, red wine vinegar, lime juice, Dijon mustard, garlic, oregano, salt, and pepper.
- Prepare a grill using medium-high heat. Skewer pieces of bell pepper, zucchini, bell onion, and chicken. Any order can be altered at your discretion.
- Place the kabobs on the hot grill and cook for 5–7 minutes on each side. After about fifteen min, when the chicken is no longer pink and the veggies have a little sear, the kabobs are done.
- Garnish with tzatziki yogurt and lemon wedges before serving.

3. Mediterranean Chicken

It's not your normal chicken supper, Mediterranean Chicken. A marinade made of yogurt, rich, warm spices, lemon juice, and fresh herbs is applied to chicken thighs. The chicken is topped off with fresh parsley, feta cheese, and served with lemon-parsley orzo after being roasted until it is moist and tender. This healthy supper will be a hit with your family!

Ingredients

CHICKEN THIGHS:

- Greek yogurt, one cup
- Olive oil, two teaspoons
- 2 pounds Chicken thighs
- Juiced from half a lemon
- 4 minced garlic cloves
- Thyme, two teaspoons of dry
- Paprika, 1 tablespoon
- Cumin, 1 1/2 tablespoons
- a half-teaspoon of dried oregano

- Optional: 1/2 teaspoon cayenne pepper
- 1 salt shakerful
- black pepper, 1/8 teaspoon

TO BE USED WITH LEMON PARSLEY ORZO:

- 16 ounces of chicken broth, vegetable broth, or plain water
- Extra virgin olive oil, three tablespoons
- 1 cup orzo
- Juiced lemon, one
- chopped one-fourth cup of fresh parsley
- a dash of pepper and salt
- For the chicken or salad, add more fresh herbs and feta cheese as a garnish.

Directions

- The oven should be heated to 425 F.
- Lay the chicken thighs out in a row on a long chopping board or place them in a big bowl. Chicken thighs should be liberally sprinkled with salt and pepper on both sides before being placed in two 9 x 13 oven dishes.
- In a medium bowl, mix together the yogurt, olive oil, lime juice, garlic, thyme, cayenne, cinnamon, basil, chili powder, salt, and pepper.
- The chicken thighs should have sauce on both the front and back. Bake the chicken thighs for between 35 and 40 minutes, or so until they reach an internal temperature of 165 degrees F.
- While the chicken is baking, boil liquid or vegetable broth for the orzo following the directions on the package. When the orzo is done, drain this and put it in a big mixing bowl.
- Mix the orzo with the lemon juice, parsley, olive oil, and salt and pepper to taste. Blend well. When the chicken is cooked through, remove it from the oven, top it with feta cheese and fresh parsley, and then serve it with the lemon-parsley orzo. Enjoy!

4. Turkey Chili

Healthy chili in the Mediterranean style, cooked with beans, ground turkey, and homemade chili seasoning. Because it's the best chili recipe they've ever had, my friends refer to it as award-winning.

Ingredients

To make your own chili powder:

- paprika sweet, 2 tablespoons
- smoked paprika, 1 teaspoon
- 1/9 cup cumin
- 1 and a half teaspoons of dried oregano
- black pepper freshly grated

To make the chili:

- turkey breast ground to 1 pound (450 grams)
- Olive oil, two tablespoons
- 1 big, chopped onion
- 400g pureed tomatoes
- 100g red kidney beans
- 1 minced garlic clove
- 1 cup chicken broth
- 1 tablespoon honey or maple syrup
- chopped green pepper, half
- 1 chopped red pepper
- ½ cup frozen sweet corn
- Sliced Kalamata olives in a cup

For the garnishes:

- Greek strained yogurt, red pepper flakes, and minced green onions

Directions

- To sauté the ground turkey, add the olive oil to a large pan that has been heated over high heat. Don't stir; let the meat brown thoroughly (this will develop some flavor). Stir to break up any lumps after the meat is a deep brown color. Cook until all liquid has been consumed.

- Combine onion, garlic, & chili powder to make chili. Cook 2–3 minutes, turning often, until the onion is shiny. Beans, carrots, honey, jalapenos, olives, and chicken broth.

- After boiling, simmer. Cover the chili and cook until thick (about 40-60 minutes). Cook corn and basil for 2 to 3 minutes more. Top with cream, scallions, & red pepper flakes.

5. Chicken Skillet with Mushrooms and Slivered Parmesan

This tasty and adaptable chicken skillet recipe includes mushrooms and slivered parmesan. The taste combination in this dish is tried and true, whether you're searching for a quick recipe for lunch or something to take center stage at the dinner table. Cooking the chicken breast in white wine and extra virgin olive oil, two components of the Mediterranean diet, results in juicy, tender chicken breast.

Ingredients

- 1.5 lbs. of chicken breast
- Extra virgin olive oil, 3 tablespoons
- Balsamic vinegar, 1 tablespoon
- 1/2 teaspoon salt
- 1/2 teaspoon pepper
- Dry thyme, 1 teaspoon
- white wine, 1/4 cup
- Round slices of 1 onion
- Sliced Portobello mushrooms, 10 ounces
- A half-cup of vegetable broth
- 1-2 ounces of thinly sliced parmesan from a block

Directions

- Strip the chicken breast into 1/2" pieces. Place in bowl. White wine, thyme, 1 tablespoon olive oil, 14 teaspoons each of salt and pepper, balsamic vinegar, and all of the above. Chicken should be thoroughly mixed, then marinated for a short time.

- Add 2 olive oil tablespoons to the skillet. The onions should be added to the pan and then sautéed for one minute on medium heat. Add 1/4 teaspoon each one of both salt and pepper, along with the mushrooms and vegetable broth, to the pan. Give mushrooms the appropriate amount of cooking time.

- After removing both mushrooms & onions from the skillet, add the chicken and marinate. Give one side two minutes to fry. Cook by flipping until finished. Add the mushrooms and onions again to the pan. Serve hot. On top, sprinkle some parmesan slices.

6. Mediterranean Turkey Meatloaf

A simple Trim Healthy Mama main dish that the whole family will enjoy is Mediterranean Turkey Meatloaf. Serve it with your preferred sides for a nutritious meal you'll prepare time and time again.

Ingredients

For the meatloaf:

- Extra lean ground turkey
- One big egg
- 1 zucchini, finely chopped, and wrung of extra moisture
- 1 medium onion, diced finely
- 1 green pepper, diced finely
- 5 tablespoons of oats for rapid cooking
- One prepared teaspoon of mustard
- Dried oregano, two tablespoons
- Italian seasoning, 1/2 teaspoon
- One-half teaspoon of dried garlic powder
- 0.5 teaspoons of salt
- 1/4 cup of feta cheese in crumbles

To make the sauce:

- Tomato paste, two tablespoons
- 1 teaspoon of water

- Optional: 1 tablespoon honey; alternately, use 1 additional tablespoon of tomato sauce and a teaspoon of your preferred sweetener.
- to taste salt

Directions

- To prepare the meat mixture, combine all of the meatloaf's components in a large bowl, excluding the feta cheese. Mix well!
- The meatloaf's form: the oven to 350 degrees Fahrenheit. Make a baking sheet lined. Shape the meat mixture into a loaf and place it on the baking pan. Create a long well in the center and fill it with cheese. As you tightly shape the meatloaf, cover the cheese with it.
- When baking, combine all the sauce ingredients in a small bowl. The meatloaf should be covered with 1/3. It takes 30 minutes to bake the meatloaf. Add another third of the sauce to the brush. Finish baking for about 20 minutes or until 165°F is reached internally. After taking it out of the oven, brush it with the leftover sauce.
- Slice and serve the loaf once it has rested for five minutes.

7. Moroccan Lamb Stew

This recipe contains all the ingredients you need to produce the tastiest lamb stew Warm Moroccan aromas and a braised lamb dish that is comfortingly soft and falls apart in your mouth. This recipe includes directions for both a pressure cooker and a crock pot.

Ingredients

- Greek Extra Virgin Private Reserve Olive Oil
- a single, chopped big yellow onion
- 3 cubed carrots
- 6 small potatoes, peeled, diced, and season with kosher salt and pepper
- 2.5 pounds of cubed, fat-trimmed American lamb with no bones (Or American lamb shoulder, bones removed, fat-trimmed)
- 3 large, roughly chopped garlic cloves
- Apricots, dried, in a cup

- 1-stick of cinnamon
- Bay leaf, one
- 1 1/2 teaspoons ground allspice
- Moroccan spice mixture ras el hanout, 1 1/2 teaspoon
- 12 tsp. of ginger, ground
- 6 canned plum tomatoes, chopped in half
- Low-sodium beef broth, 2 1/2 cups
- 15-ounce can of chickpeas

Directions

- In a large Dutch ovens (affiliate) or heavy stove pot, heat 2 tablespoons each of olive oil over medium heat until shimmering but not smoking. The potatoes, carrots, and onions should be sautéed for around 4 minutes in the hot oil. Salt and pepper the mixture after including the garlic. Remove from the saucepan, and then quickly set aside.
- If additional oil is required, add it to the same saucepan and thoroughly brown the lamb there. Add salt and pepper to taste. Return the sautéed vegetables to the pot and increase the heat to medium-high. Stir in the spices, dried apricots, bay leaf, cinnamon stick, and other ingredients. After adding the plum tomatoes and stock, bring the mixture to a boil for about five minutes.
- Cover and bake at 350 degrees Fahrenheit for 1 1/2 hours, adding water or stock if needed. Cover and bake for 30 minutes more. Remove from oven and serve with pita, couscous, Lebanese grains, or rustic bread. As an appetizer for this substantial meal, try fattoush. Enjoy!

8. Slow-roasted Mediterranean lamb

Try Curtis Stone's slow-roasted Mediterranean lamb, which is paired with a zingy oregano sauce and warm Turkish bread for simple entertaining.

Ingredients

- 250 ml or 1 cup of olive oil
- 1/4 cup finely minced fresh oregano
- 1 tablespoon of minced garlic
- Juiced from 1 lemon with finely grated zest
- 3/4 teaspoon dried red pepper flakes
- 20g fresh stems of rosemary
- 1 roast entire bone-in leg of lamb (about 2.5kg)
- 3/4 cup (185 ml) of chicken stock with less salt
- Turkish bread warmed up for serving

Directions

- Make shallow slits all over the lamb with a small, sharp knife. Oil, oregano, garlic, lemon zest, chili flakes, 1 1/4 teaspoons salt, and 3/4 teaspoons pepper should all be combined in a small bowl.
- In the middle of a sizable, heavy roasting pan, place the rosemary stalks. Salt the lamb thoroughly, and then rub it with 1/4 cup of the oregano marinade. Save the remaining oregano marinade to use as a sauce.
- The lamb on top of the rosemary. Serve lamb with a one-hour marinade at room temperature. Set the oven to 140°C (120C fan-forced).
- Cook for 1 1/2 - 1 3/4 hours, or until an immediate thermometer registers 54C for medium-rare.
- Raise the temperature of the oven to 250C (230C fan-forced). Place the lamb on a big platter. Roasting pan should be heated to medium on the stove. With a wooden spatula, scrape the browned bits from the roasting pan's bottom before adding the liquid. Into a

tall container, strain the mixture. Allow the fat to collect at the container's top before spooning it off. Keep heated after adding salt and pepper to the pan sauce.

- Place lamb in the center of a roasting pan after cleaning it. Roast lamb for 10 to 15 minutes, or until it is crisp and browned. Lamb should rest for 15 minutes before carving.

- The oregano salsa that was put aside should have three tablespoons of lime juice added to it. Carving the lamb and serving it with bread, pan dressing, and oregano sauce are both recommended.

9. Mediterranean Lamb Chops

Mediterranean lamb chops are tender and savory, with each mouthful containing hints of oregano, garlic, and lemon.

Ingredients

- 8 lamb chops, dry-rubbed
- salt and pepper as desired
- Garlic Powder, 1 tbsp.
- 1-tablespoon Lemon Pepper
- 3 tbsp. olive oil
- Lemon juice, half
- 4 minced garlic cloves
- Dry oregano, 1 tablespoon
- 1 tbs grape seed
- Alternatively, you may grill these lamb chops.

Directions

- Sprinkle lamb chops with salt, pepper, garlic salt, and lemon pepper. Wet marinade: olive oil, lime juice, garlic, oregano. Put the lamb chops in a zip lock bag and add the marinade, making sure to rub the marinade into each chop. For optimal results, marinate this overnight but at least for four hours. Seal the bag.

- Remove lamb shanks from the fridge 30 min before cooking to relax the muscles and tenderize the meat. Avocado or grapes seed oil in a nonstick pan.

- That once pan is hot, add the pork chops without overcrowding. A quick spatula press will sear the lamb chop. 5 minutes per side, or until done. Get a delicious, well-seared lamb chop. Add potatoes and/or salad for a complete dinner.

10. Dutch oven Beef Stew

The definition of comfort food is my Dutch Oven Mediterranean Beef Stew. It is a one-pot dish that can be eaten on its own and features cubes of beef that have been cooked in a rich tomato sauce with fresh veggies and herbs until they are meltingly soft.

Ingredients

- 1 kilogram of stewing beef
- 1 teaspoon coarse sea salt for cooking
- 1/2 teaspoon freshly ground black pepper
- 3 teaspoons of olive oil
- A single huge brown or yellow onion, diced.
- 4 garlic cloves, coarsely chopped
- 800 g (28 ounces) of crushed tomatoes in a can
- 250 ml (about 1 cup) of beef stock
- 3 teaspoons coarsely chopped fresh rosemary
- 1/4 teaspoon optional red pepper flakes
- 2 large courgettes or zucchini cut into pieces 1 cm wide.
- 2 huge red capsicum/bell peppers, sliced into squares of 2 12 cm (1 inch).
- 1/2 cup pitted Kalamata olives
- 3 tablespoons of freshly chopped, roughly divided, sea salt, and black pepper, to taste, fresh parsley
- Mashed potatoes, rice, crusty bread, pasta, noodles, and green salad.

Directions

- Purchase pre-cut meat or cut your own meat into 3 ½cm (1 ¼") cubes. Utilizing paper towels, pat dry the beef cubes. When the meat is seared, this will aid in the formation of a lovely brown crust. Add salt and pepper to the beef.
- In a large, heavy-based Dutch oven or skillet with a tight-fitting lid, heat 2 tablespoons of oil over high heat. Oil shouldn't burn or smoke. When the oil starts to shimmer, you will know it is hot and ready for use.

- To the pan, add 1/3 of the beef. The meat needs to be thoroughly browned on all sides. Put the meat on a platter and reserve it. Repeat with remaining beef, adding oil as necessary. Lower the temperature. If more oil is needed, add it. After adding the onion, continue to sauté it for about two minutes while stirring it occasionally. Next, add the garlic and simmer for an additional minute, stirring frequently to prevent the garlic from burning.

- Juices and all, add the cooked beef back to the pan. Add the rosemary, tomatoes, beef stock, and chili flakes (if using). Good stirring

- Bring to a simmer, cover, and cook for 1 1/2 to 2 hours, or until the beef is almost perfectly soft. Reduce the heat if necessary so the meat barely bubbles. Stir well after adding the zucchini and pepper then replace the lid. For 30 minutes, cook. If required, add a little water and stir again halfway through.

- Add 2 tablespoons of parsley as well as the olives. Check the seasoning and, if necessary, add more salt, pepper, or chili flakes. Serve family-style in the pan it was cooked in or transfer to a serving plate. Just before serving, add more parsley. Serve with buttered noodles, rice, mashed potatoes, or crusty toast.

11. Beef Cacciatore

One of the most well-known traditional original Italian dishes is cacciatore, which is Italian for "hunter." After a productive day in the woods, hunters would enjoy this straightforward dish. Since tomatoes were introduced to Italy from the New World, beef cacciatore was initially served without tomatoes. Tomatoes and bell peppers create a richer, more delicious Mediterranean sauce for this rendition of beef cacciatore.

Ingredients

- 1 pound of beef, thinly sliced (chuck roast is a good choice)
- Extra virgin olive oil, 1/4 cup
- 1 chopped onion
- 1 cup tomato sauce
- 2 chopped red peppers
- Salt to taste
- 1 chopped orange pepper
- Your choice of cooked or prepared rice, regular or gluten-free spaghetti

Directions

- When a saucepan is medium-hot after adding olive oil, add the meat and brown it well. For one minute, add the onions and sauté. In addition, tomato sauce, seasoned to taste with salt and pepper. Simmer for a while. For around 40 minutes, simmer the beef under cover until it is cooked.

- While keeping the meat in the pot, remove most of the pepper sauce and purée in a food processor. Re-add to the saucepan, stirring continuously for an additional five minutes of simmering. Serve with the pasta of your choice (can use gluten free pasta or rice as well)

12. Mediterranean Steak and Potatoes

The best and easiest recipe for Mediterranean steak!

Ingredients

- a pound of tiny red potatoes
- Extra virgin olive oil, 5 teaspoons
- 1 sliced onion
- 1/8 teaspoon freshly chopped thyme
- Salt that is kosher and freshly ground pepper
- 2 ripe tomatoes on the vine
- 1,500-calorie flat-iron steaks (2 to 3 steaks)
- 10 Kalamata olives with pits
- a half-cup of fresh parsley
- Red wine vinegar, 1 teaspoon
- 1/8 teaspoon of orange zest, grated finely

Directions

- Set the oven to 450 degrees. Place the potatoes on a microwave-safe pan, and heat for 6 to 8 minutes, flipping the potatoes halfway through. In a medium skillet that is ovenproof, bring one tablespoon of olive oil up to temperature on medium-high heat. The thyme, onion, salt, & pepper should be added according to personal preference.

- Cook for three to four minutes, tossing the mixture occasionally, or until the onion has developed a brown color.
- Rounds of tomato and potato slices should be 1/4 inch thick. Salt and pepper to taste; gently stir in a bowl with 2 tablespoons of olive oil. On top of the onion, arrange in overlapping layers (it need not be tidy). Put the dish in the oven and bake it for about 30 min, or until the tubers are cooked through and the tomatoes have wrinkled and dried up.
- While you wait, season both sides of the steaks with salt and pepper. Prepare the sauce by heating one tablespoon of olive oil in a large skillet over medium heat. Add the steak and cook them for five to six minutes each side to achieve a medium rare doneness.
- Olives and parsley should be finely chopped before being combined with the vinegar, orange zest, and remaining 1 tablespoon of olive oil. Serve the roasted veggies alongside the steak, which has been cut against the grain and divided among plates.

13. Easy Potato Omelet

Middle Eastern spices and fresh herbs in a baked potato frittata before frying the eggs, season them with salt, then stir in a little baking powder for a fluffy potato omelet. Use sweet or russet potatoes instead of gold potatoes, if you prefer.

Ingredients

- 1 to 2 rounds of green onions, both the white and green parts.
- Aleppo pepper, one teaspoon
- a half-teaspoon of sweet paprika
- 1/4 teaspoon of turmeric
- Oil from extra virgin olives
- Two minced garlic cloves
- Six big eggs
- 1/2 cup freshly chopped dill
- 1/2 cup finely minced fresh parsley

Directions

- Heat the oven to 375 degrees F and adjust the center rack. About 2 tablespoons of extra virgin olive oil are heated over medium-high heat until shimmering but not smoking in a 10-inch cast iron or oven-safe skillet.
- Garlic, green onions, and potato cubes should all be added. Add kosher salt, turmeric, paprika, coriander, and Aleppo pepper to the seasoning mixture. Cook for approximately 5 to 10 minutes, stirring frequently, or until the potatoes are soft and cooked through (manage your heat to make sure the garlic does not burn).
- The eggs and fresh herbs should be whisked together in a mixing basin. If desired, add a generous pinch of kosher salt as well as a small amount (approximately 14 tsp) of baking powder.
- Watch for the edges and bottom to slightly settle after pouring the egg mixture over the potatoes in the skillet (about 3 to 4 minutes or so).
- After heating the oven, place the skillet inside. When the eggs are completely cooked through and the top is no longer runny, bake the potato omelette for 8 to 10 minutes.

14. Pastilla Skillet Chicken Pie

Flaky phyllo pastry and a soft, strongly spiced chicken filling with warm North African tastes, such as Ras El Hanout, are used to make this savory chicken pie. Make the flavorful chicken filling a day in advance and store it in the refrigerator if you want to go ahead. Served alone, with roasted vegetables, a Moroccan-style carrot salad, or another substantial salad like my Mediterranean bean salad, pastilla is delectable.

Ingredients

- 2 lbs of skinless, boneless chicken thighs
- Salt with black pepper kosher
- Oil from extra virgin olives
- 1 large yellow onion, thinly sliced after being cut in half
- 2 minced garlic cloves
- 6 sliced and pitted medjool dates
- 1/3 cup toasted, sliced almonds
- Chopped parsley, 1/2 cup

- 3 beaten eggs
- 10 phyllo dough sheets

Spice Blend:

- Ras El Hanout, two tablespoons
- One cinnamon teaspoon
- 1/2 teaspoon of ginger, ground
- Red pepper flakes, 1/2 teaspoon
- 1/4 teaspoon of turmeric

Directions

- After wiping the chicken dry with paper towels, season both sides of the chicken with kosher salt and black pepper. A large pan is prepared for heating on medium-high heat, and two teaspoons of extra virgin olive oil are added to the pan. Add the chicken and cook it until both sides are browned (about 5 minutes or so). Chicken should now be removed from the pan and placed aside.

- Sliced onion and minced garlic should be added to the same pan, along with additional olive oil if necessary. To finish off the seasoning, sprinkle on a good amount of kosher salt. Cook until softened while frequently stirring over medium heat.

- Reintroduce the chicken pack to the pan after bringing to a boil. Cook the chicken for 10 to 15 minutes at medium-high heat, or until it is thoroughly cooked and the liquid has decreased by half.

- Add the beaten eggs to the liquid in the pan. Stir to incorporate before adding the chicken back to the pan. Add the parsley, dates, and almonds that have been chopped. Take the food off the heat Set a rack in the center and heat the oven to 375 degrees F. Brush extra virgin olive oil on the bottom and sides of a 10-inch pie plate or heat-safe pan.

- Fold one phyllo dough sheet in half vertically by taking it (the long way). Apply olive oil and place the folded phyllo sheet in the center of the pan with the sides hanging over the sides. Repeat the process with 7 more phyllo sheets, folding and brushing each sheet with oil as you go. Over the phyllo, distribute the chicken mixture. Make sure to brush each layer with olive oil before covering with the final 2 phyllo sheets. Apply extra virgin olive oil over the top.

- After fifteen to twenty minutes of baking in the center rack of the a preheated oven, the phyllo should be completely cooked and golden brown. Make sure to move the pan every so often to ensure that it bakes evenly and that it gets a uniform colour on all sides.

15. Eggs Fra Diavolo

My version of eggs in purgatory, these spicy eggs are excellent for brunch or dinner. Hardboiled eggs should be the first thing you cook. After the whites are quickly sauteed in extra virgin olive oil until they are crispy and golden brown, immerse the eggs in the savory, hot tomato sauce! See the notes for the option to cook your eggs straight in the sauce if you'd prefer to make a more traditional "eggs in purgatory."

Ingredients

- Oil from extra virgin olives
- 6 peeled hard-boiled eggs
- Regarding the hot tomato sauce
- 1 medium yellow or red onion, diced
- 5 minced garlic cloves
- 1 chopped spicy pepper, preferably a jalapeno
- Salz kosher
- diced fire-roasted tomatoes in a 15-ounce can
- 1/fourth cup tomato paste
- Dried oregano, two tablespoons
- 1 to 2 teaspoons of Aleppo pepper or dried red pepper flakes, adjusted to taste (if you like the sauce hot, you can add more)
- 1/2 cup chopped parsley or basil

Directions

- About 2 tablespoons of extra virgin olive oil should be heated to shimmer in a 10-inch skillet or pan. Add the pre-boiled eggs carefully, and fry them until the egg whites start to crisp up and turn golden brown on both sides (use a splatter guard over your pan to keep the oil from splashing). The eggs should now be removed from the pan and placed on a plate or bowl.
- In the same pan, sauté the onions, cloves, and jalapenos until the onions are translucent. Cook for three to five minutes, stirring often, until the aroma is released. To finish off the seasoning, sprinkle on a good amount of kosher salt.

- Tomato paste, diced tomatoes, and roughly 1/4 cup of water should all be added. Add one more generous dash of kosher salt to the dish. If using, add the oregano and red pepper flakes.

- When the tomato sauce is simmering, add the eggs, and cook for an additional three minutes, or until the eggs are warm.

Chapter 5

Fish and seafood Recipes

The Mediterranean diet and consuming the Mediterranean way emphasize fish and other seafood. You can find the best fish recipes and seafood recipes in the Mediterranean Dishes section below. These are simple dishes that are bursting with flavor from the region.

1. Grilled Sardines

Ingredients

- 2 large packs of trimmed baby arugula
- 16 new gills, innards, and sardines
- Extra virgin olive oil, 2 teaspoons
- The sea salt
- freshly ground black pepper
- Lemon wedges as decoration

Directions:

- Set up a burner skillet or an outdoor fire cook.
- Rinse arugula under running water, shake off extra moisture, arrange it on a platter, and store in a cool, dry place.
- Rinse the sardines in water, rub the scales off, pat them dry, and combine with the extra virgin olive oil in a large dish.
- Throw and cover. Grill the sardines until they are beautifully natural and fresh, which should take about 3 minutes per side.
- Season with sea salt and pepper, and then quickly transfer to a dish that has been prepared with arugula. Quickly serve garnished with lemon wedges.

2. Roasted Fish

Ingredients

- 1 tbsp. olive juice
- 4 smashed garlic cloves and 1 (14 oz) can of drained artichoke hearts
- One green ring pepper thinly sliced.
- 1/2 cup pitted olives that have been partitioned;
- 1 tbsp. A fennel seed
- ½ lb. quartered cod
- 4 ½ tsp. 2 tbsp. of ground orange strip worn-out adventures
- 1/3 to 1/2 cup freshly squeezed oranges, crushed pepper
- A salt press

Directions

- Heat your grill to 450 degrees.
- In the preheated skillet, arrange the artichoke hearts, garlic, ring pepper, olives, tomatoes, and fennel seeds.
- Place the fish on top of the veggies and sprinkle with salt, pepper, capers, orange peel, and orange strip.

3. Baked Fish

Ingredients

- Extra virgin olive oil, 2 teaspoons one enormously sliced onion
- 1-tablespoon orange punch
- 1/4 cup orange pieces
- Lemon juice, 1/4 cup
- 3/4 cup apple, smashed
- 1 minced garlic clove
- 1 (16 oz.) can of whole, drained, and finely chopped tomatoes with juice retained
- 1/2 cup contained tomato juice. Unbroken leaf
- 1/2 teaspoon dry basil, crushed
- Crushed dry thyme, 1/2 teaspoon
- Crushed dry oregano, 1/2 teaspoon Crushed fennel seeds, 1 teaspoon A little black peppercorn
- 1 pound of fish fillets (perch, battle, or sole)

Directions

- The onion should be cooked in the oil for about 5 minutes, or until soft. Combine all of the extra garnishes with the fish.
- Cook in the open for around 30 minutes. Arrange the fish in a heated plate and pour the sauce over it.

4. Greek Salmon Burgers

Ingredients

- 1 large egg white and 1 pound of diced skinless salmon fillets
- 1/2 cup of panko
- Crush one sea salt.
- 1/4 teaspoon freshly ground dark pepper
- 1/2 cup slices of cucumber
- 1/4 cup feta cheddar crumbles
- 4 (2.5 ounces) dry toasted bread rolls

Directions

- Using a food processor, combine the fish, egg white, and panko, and process the mixture until the fish is finely diced. Create four patties of four inches in diameter out of the fish mixture, then season them with pepper and sea salt.
- Increase the heat of the stove to medium-high, and then cook the patties for about 7 minutes per side, rotating once.

5. Garlic Shrimp with Arugula Pesto

Ingredients

- 2 cups of thinly sliced arugula
- 1/2 cup of basil leaves, lightly packed
- Walnuts, 1/4 cup
- Olive oil, 3 tablespoons three large garlic cloves
- Parmesan cheese, grated, in 2 tablespoons
- freshly squeezed lemon juice, 1 tbsp 1 package (10 ounces) of zucchini noodles
- a cooked, shelled 8 ounces (227 g) of shrimp 2 diced Roma tomatoes

Directions

- In a food processor, blend the arugula, basil, walnuts, garlic, Parmesan cheese, and lemon juice until thoroughly combined. Scrape down the sides as necessary.
- A skillet should be heated to medium. Add the cooked shrimp, zucchini noodles, and pesto. The sauce should be combined with the noodles and shrimp before being heated thoroughly.
- Good seasoning Serve with the diced tomatoes on top.

6. Grilled Whole Sea Bass

Ingredients

- 1 entire lavraki weighing 1 lb.
- Chopped fresh parsley, 1/4 cup 2 teaspoons of garlic, minced
- Rounds of one tiny lemon, 1/4 inch wide

Directions:

- Heat a grill to a high temperature.
- Olive oil should be applied to the fish's surface and the cavity in the middle. Place the thyme, parsley, garlic, and lemon slices within the cavity. On the grill, place the lavraki (see Cooking tip). Per side, cook for 6 minutes.
- Take off the tail, backbone, and head. For serving, carve 2 fillets from each side.

7. Pan-Cooked Fish with Tomatoes

Ingredients

- Extra virgin olive oil, 112 cups 12-ounces of tomato juice

- 2 organic 12-ounce cans of tomato paste 2 tablespoons each of sea salt and cane sugar Black pepper, 1 teaspoon

- 1 tsp. dried oregano from Greece 3-pound portions of fresh white fish 2 substantial sweet onions

- White wine, one cup

- Breadcrumbs, 1 1/2 cups 4 cloves of garlic

- fresh parsley, half a cup

- 4 substantial tomatoes

Directions

- The oven should be heated to 325°F. Salt, sugar, pepper, oregano, tomato paste, and olive oil should all be combined. Rub a little amount of the mixture into the bottom of a roasting pan about 9 by 13 inches.

- Alongside one another, arrange the fresh fish fillets on top of the tomato mixture. Slices of onion should be placed on top, overlapping.

- Each piece of fish should have a uniform coating of wine. Over the fish, pour half of the tomato-olive oil mixture. Combine parsley, garlic, and bread crumbs. Cover the fish with.

- Over the fish, arrange the tomato slices in an overlapping pattern. The leftover tomato mixture should be drizzled on top. For 40 to 45 minutes, bake.

8. Steamed Fish with Veggies

Ingredients

- two lemons juice
- Extra virgin olive oil, 4 tablespoons Sea salt, two tablespoons
- 1/4 cup chopped Kalamata olives,
- freshly ground black pepper, 1 teaspoon 4 fish fillets (6 to 8 ounces each)
- 1/2 pound chopped tomatoes
- 1/2 cup finely chopped scallions
- Fennel bulb, one

Directions

- Turn the oven on to 375°F. Rub salt, pepper, two tablespoons of olive oil, lemon juice, and salt together. Add the fish and marinate for 10 minutes in the fridge.
- Combine the tomatoes, scallion, olives, capers, vinegar, 2 tablespoons of remaining olive oil, and garlic in a medium bowl.
- Using four sheets of parchment paper measuring 12 by 16 inches folded in half, cut out a half-heart shape while preserving as much parchment as you can. To create a bed for the fish, unfold the hearts and insert a quarter of the fennel near the center crease.
- Beginning at the bottom end, fold the edges over one another to seal the package before folding the paper back over the fish. For 20 minutes, bake.

9. Monkfish stuffed

Ingredients

- 4 fresh white fish fillets, each 6 ounces
- 1/2 tsp. sea salt
- freshly ground black pepper, half a teaspoon
- 4 feta cheese cubes
- Minced green olives in 1/4 cup
- 1/4 cup orange pulp, minced 1/2 teaspoon dried dill and 1 tablespoon orange zest
- Chopped fresh Greek basil, 1/4 cup

Directions

- 2 tablespoons of olive oil, salt, and pepper are blended with the fish. Combine the feta, olives, and orange pulp in a separate bowl. Spread the mixture over the fish fillets to cover them. Roll the fillets and secure them together by sticking two toothpicks through to the opposite side.
- Heat the remaining olive oil in a large skillet over medium-high heat for about 15 seconds. Depending on their thickness, add the rolled fillets and cook for 6 to 8 minutes, turning them over halfway through. Sprinkle an equal amount of orange zest, dill, and basil on top of each serving.

10. Santorinian shrimp

Ingredients

- 1 lb. of shrimp
- Extra virgin olive oil, 5 teaspoons 2 teaspoons of salt, kosher
- 4 minced garlic cloves
- 2 pounds of tomatoes, grated or chopped
- 1/2 tsp. red pepper flakes
- 1/2 teaspoon dried oregano from Greece feta cheese, 6 ounces
- 3 tablespoons freshly chopped parsley

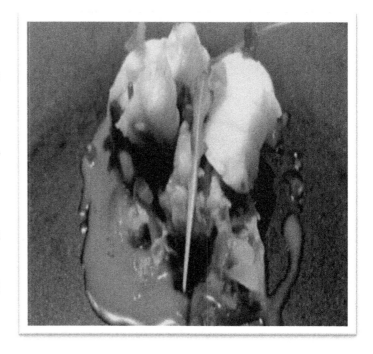

Directions

- Set the oven to 400°F. Salt the onion and then add it. For 3 to 5 minutes, cook. Pepper and garlic are added. For 4 minutes, cook. Cook the tomatoes, oregano, and red pepper flakes for 10 minutes.
- Spread the feta crumbles on top. For 10 to 12 minutes, bake.

11. Cocktail Shrimp

Ingredients

- 20 to 30 count wild shrimp, weighing one pound 1 egg
- 2 teaspoons minced dill or Greek oregano, 1 tablespoon
- Olives from Kalamata 1 minced garlic clove
- Few ground black pepper
- 1 tablespoon of mustard
- 1/2 cup of walnut oil

Directions

- Put a pot with 8 cups of water over high heat.

- Boil the shrimp for two to three minutes, or until pink. Cool and drain.

- Combine the egg, oregano, olives, garlic, and mustard in a food processor. To mingle, blend.

- The walnut oil should be added very gradually into the feed tube of your food processor while it is operating at low speed.

- Add the salt and pepper once it has thickened to a consistency resembling mayonnaise. Serve.

12. Stuffed Squid

Ingredients

Squid

- Extra virgin olive oil, 1 tablespoon one sliced onion

- sea salt, one teaspoon

- freshly ground black pepper, 1 teaspoon 3 minced garlic cloves

- 1 lb. small squid

- 12 pounds of halved cherry tomatoes

- 14 cups washed basmati or long-grain rice

- roasted pine nuts, 14 cup

- 14 cups of basil, fresh

Sauce

- Extra virgin olive oil, 1/4 cup one sliced onion

- sea salt, one teaspoon

- Black pepper, 1 teaspoon 2 chopped garlic cloves

- 4 ml of dry white wine

- 28-ounce can of chopped tomatoes, one

- 1 lemon juice 14 cups chiffonade-cut fresh basil

- Slices of lemon for serving

Directions

Squid

- Heat the olive oil in a pot on a medium-high heat setting. For five minutes, sauté onion with salt and pepper.
- Tentacles from the squid should be chopped up and added to the stew at this time. Rice, pine nuts, and cherry tomatoes should be added. For three minutes.
- Incorporate the chopped basil into the mixture. With a toothpick, prick the squid bodies all over, and then cut off the very tip of the hollow.
- Fill each squid about one-fourth and one-half full. Make sure there is space since the rice will expand while the squid cooks in the sauce.

Sauce

- The olive oil should be heated over medium-high heat in the same saucepan that you used to cook the stuffing.
- Add the salt, pepper, and onion. For three to five minutes. Include the garlic. For about one minute, cook.
- Deglaze the pan by stirring white wine. Add the tomatoes and stir. For 10 minutes, cook. Insert the basil. To the pot, layer the stuffed squid evenly. For 30 minutes, simmer the saucepan with the cover on. If there is too much resistance when the squid is pierced with a knife, cook it for an additional 15 minutes.
- Squeeze the lemon into the pot once the squid is fully cooked, and serve with more lemon slices.

13. Octopus with Peaches and Figs

Ingredients

- Octopus tentacles weighing 1 kg.
- Extra virgin olive oil, 1/4 cup sea salt, one teaspoon
- Black pepper, 1 teaspoon
- 1 teaspoon of garlic granules
- 1/2 teaspoon dried oregano from Greece 1 cup balsamic vinegar with figs
- 6 freshly cut figs
- 2 big peaches, cut into quarters
- Chopped fresh parsley, 1/4 cup

Directions

- Mix the octopus, olive oil, salt, pepper, garlic, and oregano well to coat in a sizable bowl. Refrigerate for two hours while marinating. Before cooking, bring it to room temperature.
- Bring the fig balsamic vinegar to a boil in an 8- to 10-inch heavy-bottomed large skillet over medium-high heat. Turn down the heat to a steady simmer. Use the flat side of a metal spatula to stir so that any vinegar that has thickened mixes with the liquid rather than adhering to the pan. Add the octopus and whisk fast for about 2 to 3 minutes after the vinegar has bubbled on top for around 4 minutes.
- To the vinegar that is still in the skillet, add the figs and peaches. Just till coated and tender, toss them into the caramelized vinegar and cook for about a minute. Gently mix in the serving bowl after transfer. Add the parsley on top.

14. Seafood Rice

Ingredients

- Extra virgin olive oil, 1 tablespoon 11.2 pounds of fish
- 1 sliced onion, 1 tsp sea salt
- 1 cup chopped celery, 4 minced garlic cloves, and 2 medium tomatoes
- ½ cup of dry white wine Arborio rice, two cups
- Chopped fresh parsley, 1/4 cup
- 1/4 cup freshly chopped dill 4 cups of chicken stock

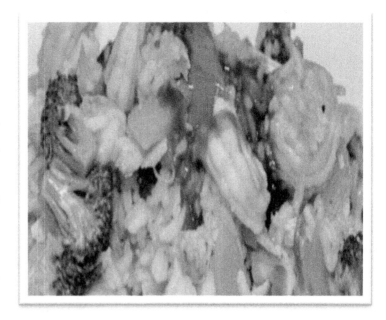

Directions

- Heat 1 tablespoon of olive oil in a pan over medium-high heat.
- Cook the squid for about two minutes after adding it. Squid removed, kept aside. Heat up the skillet with the final teaspoon of olive oil.
- Add salt and onion. For five minutes, cook.

Prepare garlic

- Tomato and celery mix for three minutes. Cook for about 3 minutes while stirring constantly after adding the wine. Rice, parsley, dill, and 4 cups of broth are all stirred in. For 15 minutes, simmer the skillet with the lid on.
- Add the shrimp and mussels to the rice mixture, cover the skillet, and simmer for an additional five minutes, or until the shrimp are barely cooked. Put the squid back in the skillet. Unopened mussels should be thrown away. Choose the lemon wedges side.

15. Mediterranean Mussels

Ingredients

- Sliced white onion and three tablespoons of olive oil
- fennel seeds, 2 tablespoons, 4 minced garlic cloves
- 1 crushed teaspoon of red pepper a dash of black pepper and salt 1 cup of poultry stock
- one teaspoon of lemon juice
- 2 1/2 pounds of cleaned mussels
- 1/2 cup chopped parsley
- 1/2 cup diced tomatoes

Directions

- Over medium-high heat, add the onion to a skillet with the oil. Add the garlic for two minutes in the pan. Except for the mussels, add the remaining ingredients, mix, and simmer for an additional 3 minutes.
- After adding the mussels and cooking the mixture for an additional 6 minutes, divide it all among bowls and serve.

Chapter 6

Vegetable mains and meatless recipes

There are so many amazing ways that veganism may enhance our quality of life, including astounding health benefits, less environmental impact, improved resource utilization, and many more. Think about the standards you uphold in yourself and the guiding principles you rely on to distinguish between good and wrong. Maintaining a substantial lifestyle change will be easier if you have absolute faith in your decision. Fortunately, vegetables are the part of the Mediterranean diet and here below are some easy recipes for you!

1. Salsa with Black Beans and Corn

You can prepare this black bean & corn salsa in a matter of minutes. It's the ideal appetizer for a get-together with friends or a side dish for just a Mexican supper.

Ingredients

- black beans, two 15-ounce cans
- 1/2 cup thawed frozen corn
- 1 medium sized, diced tomatillo
- 1/2 small red onion, sliced fine
- 1/2 cup chopped fresh cilantro leaves

Dressing

- ¼ cup juice of fresh lemons
- fresh lime juice, 1 tablespoon
- 2 teachers of honey
- half a teaspoon of sea salt
- 1/4 teaspoon brand new black pepper

Directions

- Rinse the beans thoroughly with clean water.
- The beans should be drained and put in a sizable serving bowl.
- Corn, tomatoes, red onion, & cilantro should be added. Mix thoroughly by tossing.

- The remaining ingredients for the dressing should be whipped together in a small bowl.
- Toss the salad with the dressing after drizzling it over it. Serve right away.

2. Gazpacho

A chilled summer soup called gazpacho mixes the tastes of your favorite summer veggies. Make this tasty and fresh gazpacho at home using ingredients from your garden or the nearby farmers' market.

Ingredients

- 6 Rome tomatoes, ripe and halved
- 1 seeded and chopped sweet red pepper
- one seeded and chopped green bell pepper
- one small red onion, cut into quarts
- 1 clove of peeled and sliced garlic
- organic tomato juice, 3 cups
- white wine vinegar, 1/4cup
- salt and ¼ cup an additional olive oil
- 1/4 teaspoon fresh black pepper ground

Directions

- The tomatoes should be chopped finely but not puréed after being placed in a food processor.
- Into a bowl, add the tomatoes.
- In a food processor, add the red & green peppers and pulse several times to finely chop them.
- While the onion and garlic are in the food processor, add the peppers to the bowl containing the tomatoes.
- Then, add the finely chopped onion and garlic to the bowl containing the other veggies.
- Add the salt, pepper, tomato juice, vinegar, and olive oil.
- Overnight chill the bowl with its cover; serve chilled.

3. Basil-Tomato Bisque

Tomatoes include significant quantities of iron, iron, calcium, and potassium in addition to being a great source of vitamin C. Lycopene, an antioxidant associated with cancer protection, is also present in tomatoes.

Ingredients

- 1/2 pound of rare tomatoes
- a pair of thinly sliced yellow onions
- minced garlic, 2 tablespoons
- basil leaves, 1 cup, chunked
- olive oil, 3 tablespoons
- pepper and salt
- stock of 1 cup of vegetables
- half a cup of heavy cream

Directions

- Cut the tomatoes in half after giving them a cool water rinse.
- On top of the tomatoes, scatter the chopped basil, onions, and garlic on a baking sheet with a rim.
- Sprinkle with salt and pepper and drizzle with olive oil.
- The veggies should be roasted for 20 mines, or until the tomatoes have a light sear and the onions are caramelized.
- Into a sizable stockpot, scoop the vegetables.
- Stir the mixture to a boil after adding the vegetable stock.
- Remove the soup from the heat and puree it with an immersion blender.
- After adding the whipping cream inside a steady flow, bring the soup back to a boil.
- Cook until well heated.
- Serve hot with fresh herbs leaves as a garnish.

4. Eggplant Rolls

Ingredients

- 150 ml egg plant oils, 2 pieces
- a single onion
- 2 garlic cloves
- 2 tomatoes and 0.5 pieces of the white part of a leek
- 200 ml Port wine and 3 tbsp. of tomato puree
- 1 teaspoon salt and 2 tablespoons chopped basil
- 4 Basil tickets
- 3 pinches of pepper, ground

Directions

- Slice the washed eggplant into 12 pieces lengthwise.
- Lightly cook the eggplant slices on both sides in 100 ml of oil while seasoning them with salt.
- Spread a piece of paper towel over the cooked eggplant.
- Cube up the remaining eggplant and set aside.
- Spread the minced onion and garlic over the remaining oil to glaze.
- To the onion, add the chopped leek, cubed eggplant, peeled tomatoes, tomato puree, and chopped basil. Simmer for 10 minutes to cook out as much water as you can.
- Top each slice of eggplant with about a spoonful of the stewed vegetables, and then roll it up like a roulade.
- Place the eggplant in a baking dish or baking dish, and then pour wine over the top. If there is any left over, add it as well.
- Bake the stew for 15 to 20 minutes.
- Garnish with chopped basil before serving.

5. Basil & Spinach Scramble

Ingredients

- 2/TBS of olive oil
- 4 eggs and 100g cherry tomatoes
- Milk, 60 ml.
- 200g of baby spinach, 200g of chopped basil, and black pepper

Directions

- The tomatoes are added to a pan with 1 tbsp hot oil. Beat the eggs in a jug and add the milk, black pepper, and basil while they are frying.
- Place the tomatoes on the dishes after removing them from the pan. As the eggs start to scramble, add the oil, spinach, and egg mixture to the pan. Add to the plates after it is ready, and then serve.

6. Steamed Green Beans

Ingredients

- Green beans one pounds
- Water

Directions

- If there are any ends or strings on the beans, wash them off. Cut them or leave them whole.
- They should be steamed for 10 to 15 minutes, covered, in a steamer basket over an inch or so of quickly boiling water, until they are barely soft but still crunchy.
- Drain, then season as desired.

7. Edgy Veggie Wraps

Ingredients

- 1 cucumber and 100g cherry tomatoes
- Kalamata olives, six
- 50g feta cheese, two big whole meal tortilla wraps
- 2 tbsp. of houmous

Directions

- Cut the cucumber into sticks, divide the olives, and remove the stones before chopping the tomatoes.
- The tortillas are heated. Over the wrap, spread the houmous. Roll up after placing the veggie mixture in the center.

8. Vegetable Pie

Ingredients

- 150 g of asparagus in cane 2 tablespoons of vegetable oil
- a single onion
- sugar and one teaspoon
- a single zucchini
- 2 garlic cloves
- Baby spinach, 100 g, 4 tickets, basil

- Grated parmesan, 60 grams
- 25 grams of soft cottage cheese
- Mascarpone, 250 grams
- 4 eggs
- 4 tablespoons semi-coarse flour

- 3 grinds of pepper
- 40-grated parmesan cheese
- Some mixed veggies for garnishing

Directions

- Drain the asparagus well, and then spread it out on a sieve to drip. After that, chop the asparagus into tiny pieces.
- Cube the zucchini, place it in a colander, season with salt, and let stand for 20 minutes. After rinsing with water, towel the zucchini. Set the oven's temperature to 180 ° C. Heat the oil in a big saucepan. Add the minced garlic, sugar, and onion slices, and cook for 3 minutes.
- After adding the spinach, let it disappear. Turn off the heat, stir in the basil, season with salt and pepper, and let cool.
- Grease and put coarse flour on top of baking paper to line a 20 cm diameter circular mould. In a bowl, combine the cottage cheese, mascarpone, flour, eggs, and parmesan. Stir in the asparagus, zucchini, and cooked spinach.
- Scoop the dough into the mould that has been prepared, top with Parmesan, and bake for 35 to 40 minutes. Permit the cake to cool after baking. Serve alongside a vegetable salad.

9. Grilled Eggplant

Ingredients

- 2 pieces of little egg plants 2 tbsp of oils
- Salt, 4 pinches
- Grilled Halloumi cheese, 250 grams 1 red onion slice
- 6 tbsp olive oil
- 1 tsp. of brown sugar walnuts, 50 g
- 1.5 tbsp lemon juice 1 teaspoon of honey
- Finely shredded hard cheese, 6 tablespoons
- 2/TBS of olive oil

Directions

- Combine 6 tablespoons of olive oil, honey, almonds, and lemon juice.

- Pour 2 tablespoons of oil over 2 finely chopped onions, add sugar, and stir continually until the onions caramelize. Cut the aborigines lengthwise into 12 slices, each about 1.5 cm thick. Halloumi cheese was cut into 12 blocks. Apply olive oil to both sides of the eggplant slices.

- Grill the eggplant slices for 1-2 minutes on each side over a moderately warm grill (the eggplant will still be grilled with the filling). Salt the eggplant slices, then top each with a block of cheese, a small amount of caramelized onion, and a nut combination. (Rotate the slice.)

- Grill the buns for 5 minutes or so to soften the cheese. Serve with cheese on top.

10. Couscous Vegetables

Ingredients

- 300 grams of couscous

- three tomatoes

- One cucumber salad piece and two shallots

- 4 radish chunks

- 1/2 cup of chopped parsley

- 3 pieces of sliced radish

- Olive oil, 70 ml

- White wine vinegar, 2 tablespoons Salt, two pinches

- 2 pinches of white pepper, ground

Directions

- Follow the recipe for the couscous on the package. Let the cooked couscous cool. Separate the vegetables into identically sized pieces.

- Combine parsley, chopped vegetables, and couscous. Combine the olive oil, vinegar, salt, and pepper. Drizzle the mixture over the dish.

- Gently combine, top with radish slices, and serve. Use veggie broth instead of water to make couscous.

11. Mediterranean Baked Zucchini Sticks

Ingredients

- 2 medium zucchini, sliced down the middle, lengthwise
- a cup of chopped olives
- 0.25 cup chopped tomatoes
- Dried oregano, 1 teaspoon
- 0.25 cups chopped parsley
- To taste, add salt and black pepper.
- 2 ounces of crumbled Feta cheese
- bell pepper,0.25 cup
- 1 teaspoon minced garlic, chopped

Directions

- Heat the oven to 350 degrees Fahrenheit to remove the zucchini's flesh, and use a big spoon. The flesh can be consumed or thrown away. Combine the prepared vegetables and add salt, oregano, and black pepper to taste.
- Fill each of the four zucchini "boats" with a small amount of the mixture. The zucchini boats should be arranged on a baking sheet and baked for about 15 minutes.
- After that, top with the feta cheese and broil for a further two minutes. Add fresh parsley as a garnish.

12. Quinoa & Stir-Fried Veg

Ingredients

- 1 kg of quinoa
- 3 tablespoons of olive oil
- one clove of garlic
- 2 carrots, cut finely,
- slice into skinny sticks 150g sliced leek
- 150 g of broccoli
- Chopped 50g of tomatoes into little florets.
- 100 ml of vegetable broth
- Tomato puree, 1 teaspoon
- 1/2 lemon juice

Directions

- Follow the quinoa's cooking instructions on the package. In the meantime, immediately sauté the garlic in a skillet with 3 tbsp of olive oil for 1 minute. Add the broccoli, leeks, carrots, and stir-fry for 2 minutes, or until everything is glossy.
- After combining the stock and tomato puree, add the tomatoes and stir. For 3 minutes, cook with a cover. Quinoa should be drained before adding the remaining oil and lemon juice. Place the vegetables on top after dividing them across plates.

13. Bok Choy Stir Fry

Ingredients

- bok choy, washed, in 8 cups (leaves and stalks separated)
- 1/2 cup of peanut oil
- 1 finely cut garlic clove
- freshly minced 1/4-inch slices of ginger
- a smidge of soy sauce
- Rice vinegar, two tablespoons
- 1/8 cup sugar

Directions

- Separately chop the leaves and stalks into one-inch pieces. Oil is added and a large skillet or wok is heated to a high temperature. Garlic and ginger should be added once the oil has warmed up, and they should be cooked until the garlic begins to soften.
- The stems should have somewhat softened after 4 minutes of cooking in the oil with frequent stirring. After that, swirl and toss often for an additional 2 minutes while cooking the vinegar, sugar, soy sauce, and chopped leaves. Serve them on top of rice or as a side dish with chicken or pork.

14. Steamed Carrots

Ingredients

- Baby carrots, 1 1/2 cups
- water

Directions

- Carrots should be put in a steamer basket. Bring to a boil in a saucepan over 1 inch of water till tender, 5 to 8 minutes with the cover on. Place the carrots in a bowl.

15. Crispy Kale Chips

Ingredients

- 1 head of kale completely dried after washing.
- 2 teaspoons of olive oil
- for sprinkling: sea salt

Directions

- To 275 °F, preheat the oven. Cut the kale into 112-inch sections after removing the ribs. Put on a baking pan and sprinkle with salt and olive oil.
- Bake the leaves for about 20 minutes, turning them over halfway through. Become finger food.

Chapter 7

Salads, Sides and Soups Recipes

1. White Bean Salad with Tomato & Cucumber

Ingredients

- a dash of black pepper and salt chopped 10–12 basil leaves,
- 3 cups of assorted salad greens
- 15 oz. of low-sodium cannellini beans
- 1 teaspoon mustard,
- 1 cup cherry tomatoes, cut in half
- 1/fourth cup red wine vinegar
- 2 tablespoons olive oil cukes, five, diced
- 2 tbsp. chopped onion

Directions

- Combine your basil, vinegar, olive oil, mustard, salt, and black pepper in a food processor or blender and process until it is smooth. This will serve as your clothing.
- Your salad's components, including the greens, tomatoes, cucumber, onion, and beans, should be combined in a big bowl. Mix well after adding the dressing.

2. Cannellini Bean Salad

Ingredients

- Cannellini beans, 600g
- 70g halved cherry tomatoes
- 1/2 of a finely sliced red onion
- Red wine vinegar, 1/2 tbsp
- a little clump of ripped basil

Directions

- After being rinsed and drained, combine the beans with the tomatoes, onion, and vinegar. Just before serving, the season before adding the basil.

3. Avocado Soup

This chilled avocado soup is the perfect way to cool off on a hot summer day because it is cool and creamy.

Ingredients

- avocados, 3 ripe, pitted and chopper
- two pounds of vegetable stock
- one-half cup minced red onion
- 14 cups fresh cilantro leaves, choppered
- juice of fresh lemon, 2 tablespoons
- salt, 1 teaspoon
- one cup full of milk

Directions

- In a food processor, combine the avocado, vegetable stock, red onion, cilantro, lemon juice, and salt. Pour the smoothed-out mixture into a serving basin after blending.
- For many hours, cover and refrigerate until cool. Just before serving, whisk in whole milk and top with cilantro leaves.

4. Mushroom and Kale Soup

This soup made with kale and mushrooms is the ideal balance of soft mushrooms and wilted greens.

Ingredients

- coconut oil, 1 tablespoon
- one teaspoon of mixed garlic
- 2 pounds choppered fresh mushrooms
- 1 large chopped yellow onion
- 5 cups devised low-sodium vegetable broth
- 3 poods of chopper kale, curly
- salt, 1/2 teaspoon
- 14 teaspoon brand new black pepper

Directions

- In a stockpot, heat the oil to a medium-high temperature. Cook the garlic for a minute after adding it. After 6 to 8 minutes, until the mushroom and onion are soft, stir in the ingredients.
- Bring the vegetable broth to a boil after adding it. Boil for 20 minutes on low heat.
- Add the greens, salt, and pepper, and stir. Serve hot after cooking the kale for two to three minutes, until it has wilted.

5. Spinach and Sun-dried Tomato Salad

Vitamins A, D, E, calcium, iron, potassium, and many other minerals are abundant in spinach, which is also a strong source of vegan protein. This salad has the greatest of both worlds because it is both filling and delicious.

Ingredients

- baby spinach leaves 4 cups
- 2 pockets chopper romaine leaf
- 1 cup halved cherry tomatoes
- 14 cups of red onion, thinly sliced

Dressing

- 2 drained, sun-dried tomatoes in oil
- extra-virgin olive oil, 2 tablespoons
- balsamic vinegar, 2 tablespoons
- one teaspoon of mixed garlic
- brand new black peppers

Directions

- Rinse the romaine and spinach with clean water, and then pat them dry.
- Toss thoroughly after adding the red onion and cherry tomatoes.
- In a food processor, combine the remaining ingredients.
- To prepare the dressing, pulse the ingredients twice, then blend until thoroughly incorporated and smooth.
- Toss the salad with the dressing after drizzling it over it.
- In two dishes, divide the salad.
- Add finely ground black pepper as a garnish before serving.

6. Sweet Potato with Roasted Leek Soup

Potatoes are a fantastic source of magnesium, copper, and iron. They have been demonstrated to enhance digestion and help detoxification in addition to being advantageous for eye health.

Ingredients

- 2 pounds quartered sweet potatoes
- 2 rinsed and chopped leeks (white and light-green parts only)
- 3 tablespoons divided olive oil
- one tablespoon of minced garlic
- 1 large chopped yellow onion
- low-sodium vegetable broth, 5 cups
- salt, 1 teaspoon
- fresh black pepper, 12 teaspoon
- unsweetened coconut milk, 1 cup
- turn on the 375°f

Direction

- Toss the potato and leeks together in a big bowl. Garlic and 2 tablespoons of olive oil are added, and everything is coated. On a rimmed cookie sheet, spread out the potato and leeks and roasted for approximately 30 to 40 minutes or until just faintly browned
- In a stockpot, warm the last tablespoon of olive oil over medium heat. After adding the onions, simmer for 5 minutes or until they are soft. Stir in the leeks and potatoes that have been roasted.
- Add the salt, pepper, and vegetable broth by stirring. After bringing your soup to a boil, turn off the heat and use an immersion blender to purée it. Serve hot after whisking in the coconut milk.

7. Chickpea and Chicken Salad

Ingredients

- 8–10 sliced olives
- 1 can of chickpeas (about 15 oz), diced 3–4 fresh basil leaves
- Feta cheese in crumbles and two tablespoons of olive oil
- 1 cup of shredded, cooked chicken breast
- 1 tomato and 0.5 heads of lettuce, chopped
- 1 teaspoon lime or lemon juice

Directions

- To make your salad dressing, combine the basil, lemon juice, and olive oil. The remaining ingredients for your vegetables should be combined with the dressing. If desired, season with a little salt and pepper.

8. Bean Soup

Protein and dietary fiber are both present in lentils in good amounts. They work well together with the tomatoes and soft onions in this dish, which also includes garlic and powdered cumin.

Ingredients

- dry lentils, 1 pound
- two teaspoons of olive oil
- one teaspoon of mixed garlic

- 1 chopped yellow onion
- 1 chopped large stalk of celery
- salt, 1 teaspoon
- a teaspoon of black pepper, 1/4
- one cup of sliced tomatoes

Directions

- Low-sodium vegetables, 8 cups 12 teaspoon ground cumin
- Lentils should be rinsed in clean water, drained, and set aside.
- In a stockpot set over medium heat, heat the olive oil.
- Cook the garlic for a minute after adding it.
- Add the onion & celery, add salt and pepper, then simmer for 6 to 8 minutes, or until the vegetables are soft.
- Bring the soup to a boil after adding the lentils, tomatoes, vegetable broth, and ground cumin.
- During 35 to 40 minutes, simmer the stew, covered, over low heat.
- With an immersion blender, remove the stew from the heat and purée; then, warmly serve.

9. Salad of broccoli and almonds

Numerous vitamins and minerals, such as vitamin E, magnesium, calcium, and selenium, can be found in broccoli. Fresh broccoli's snappy texture in this dish contrasts nicely with the sharpness of shredded carrots and sliced almonds.

Ingredients

- 6 cups chopped fresh florets of broccoli
- one large diced stalk of celery
- 1 diced peeled carrot

- half green cucumber
- sesame tahini, 1/3 cup
- 3 teaspoons natural honey
- extra-virgin olive oil 1 tablespoon
- fresh lemon juice 1 tablespoon
- almonds thinly sliced 12 cup
- 1/4 cup green onions, thinly sliced

Directions

- In a bowl, mix the broccoli, onions, and carrots. Good stirring
- The ingredients for the dressing should be combined and whipped up in a bowl with the thin, honey, olives, and lemon juice.
- Toss the salad with the dressing after pouring it over it.
- Just before serving, toss in the sliced almonds and green onions.

10. A soup made with asparagus

High quantities of antioxidants and foliate found in asparagus have been proven to decrease the aging process and cognitive impairment. Additionally, it has dietary fiber, chromium, and vitamins A, C, and E.

Ingredients

- fresh asparagus spears weight 2 pounds
- 8 pools of water
- olive oil, 3 tablespoons
- tablespoons flour of rice
- 1 diced yellow onion
- one teaspoon of mixed garlic
- only white & light-green parts of 1 cup of chopped leeks
- pepper and salt

Directions

- Cut the asparagus spears into 1-inch segments after trimming the ends and rinsing it in cool water. In a sizable stockpot, bring the water to a boil before adding the chopped asparagus.
- After 3 minutes of boiling, strain the asparagus and save the liquid. In a sizable saucepan set over medium-high heat, warm the olive oil. Once the flour has been incorporated, whisk in the chopped leeks, onion, and garlic.
- Stirring often, cook the mixture for 5 minutes or until the onion starts to soften. Add the saved cooking liquid and the chopped asparagus, and then simmer the mixture. To cook the asparagus, cover the broth and simmer it for about 25 minutes.
- Use an immersion blender to puree the soup after removing it from the heat. Discard the particles after straining the soup thru a mesh strainer. Salt and pepper should be whisked into the soup before adding it back to the pot. Before serving, cover the soup & chill for four to six hours, or until completely cold. Add a fresh parsley and cilantro sprig to the top of each serving.

11. Salad with Mandarin Spinach and Walnuts

Mandarin oranges are renowned for having a sweet flavor and being high in vitamin C. The oranges in this recipe offer a wonderful counterpoint to the fresh spinach's freshness and the crunch of the chopped walnuts.

Ingredients

- fresh baby spinach 4 cups
- 1 small can of drained mandarin oranges
- 14 small red onions, sliced fine
- 1/4 cup chopped nuts

Directions

- In a salad dish, mix the spinach, lemons, and red onion.
- Divide the salad between two bowls after tossing to incorporate the ingredients.
- On serve, add sliced walnuts to the top of each salad.

12. Cauliflower Soup with Cream

It is well known that cauliflower has a lot of nutrients. It is one of the vegetables with the highest nutrient density since it is packed with Vitamin b, potassium, manganese, and other minerals. Additionally, it is a fantastic source of antioxidants that enhance the liver's capacity for detoxification.

Ingredients

- two teaspoons of coconut oil
- one teaspoon of mixed garlic
- 1 small onion cut into chops
- 1chopped large stalk of celery
- salt, 1/2 teaspoon
- a teaspoon of black pepper, 1/4
- low-sodium vegetable broth 4 cups
- 1 chopped head of cauliflower

Directions

- In a big saucepan, warm the coconut oil over medium heat. Garlic is added and cooked for one minute. After adding, sauté the onion & celery for six to eight minutes, or until tender.
- Add the vegetable broth, salt, and pepper after stirring. Bring the broth to a boil after adding the cauliflower. Reduce heat, cover, and cook cauliflower for 20 to 25 minutes, or until soft.
- Remove the soup from the heat and puree it with an immersion blender. After bringing the stew to room temperature, cover it and chill it for two to four hours. Offer chilled.

13. Marinated Zucchini Salad

Ingredients

- 3 smaller zucchini, 100 milliliters of olive oil
- 3 tablespoons of lemon juice
- 1.5 tablespoons grated lemon peel
- 4 pinches of salt, 2 chopped mint sprigs, and 2
- 4 pinches of pepper, finely ground 3 pieces of peeled tomatoes
- 4 huge black olive pieces Delicious onions, 2 pieces.

Directions

- Slice the cleaned zucchini and place it in a small, square basin. Drizzle lemon juice, olive oil, and chopped mint over the zucchini. 30 minutes of cool marinating is required.
- Chop tomatoes and add them to a bowl after peeling. Slice the olives and mix them with the tomatoes. Add the diced, stem-free onion last.
- Season with pepper and salt to taste, then stir in 2 tablespoons of oil.
- Arrange the marinated zucchini pieces in an expansive dish or platter. Zucchini should be lightly peppered and salted. Position the chopped tomatoes in the center. Top with chopped onions before serving.

14. Quinoa salad

Ingredients

- 1 cup of raw white quinoa
- 0.5 teaspoons of salt
- Cucumber, chopped, seeded, and unpeeled, 1 cup
- 1 can of drained tomatoes with basil, garlic, and oregano (14.5 oz each).

- 1 can of sliced, ripe olives (2.25 oz each), drained
- 1/3 cup of feta cheese, crumbled
- 14 cups finely minced red onion

Directions

- Adding salt and cook the quinoa as directed on the package. Cucumber, drained tomatoes, olives, cheese, and onion are combined in a large bowl and put aside.
- In a 13x9-inch baking dish, spread the cooked quinoa. 5 minutes of gentle cooling in the refrigerator. Toss the quinoa lightly into the vegetable mixture to mingle. Serve right away or chill in the fridge until cool.

15. Fish Soup

Ingredients

- Cans of chicken broth (14 ounces)
- 1 (14.5 ounces) can of drained diced tomatoes
- one sliced onion
- 12 a chopped green bell pepper
- 8 ounces of tomato sauce in one can
- Orange juice, half a cup
- 0.5 cups of dry white wine
- Can of mushrooms, 2 12 ounces
- sliced black olives, 1/4 cup
- 1 bay leaf, 2
- 2 minced garlic cloves
- one tablespoon of dried basil
- 14 teaspoon crushed fennel seeds
- 1/8 teaspoon of black pepper, ground
- Medium shrimp weighing 1 pound, peeled and deveined
- 1 pound of diced cod fillets

Directions

- In a slow cooker, mix together the following ingredients: broth, tomatoes, onion, bell pepper, tomato sauce, orange juice, wine, mushrooms, olives, bay leaves, garlic, basil, fennel seed, and black pepper. Low flame for cooking.
- Cod and shrimp are combined. Cook the shrimp for a further 15 to 30 minutes, or until they are opaque. Before serving, throw away the bay leaves.

Chapter 8

Fruit, Dessert and Snack Recipes

1. Avocado Apple Breakfast Smoothie

Ingredients

- 1 Avocado
- 1 teaspoon of honey
- 1 banana, 2 12 tbsp chia seeds
- 2 glasses of water 1 chopped apple
- three cups spinach

Directions

- Place everything in the blender and process until smooth. Immediately serve and savor.

2. Frozen Fruit Salad with Mint

Ingredients

- 1 cup of strawberries, frozen
- Frozen peaches, 1 cup
- 1 cup of mango frozen
- 1 cup of blueberries, frozen
- 1-tablespoon lemon juice
- 2 tablespoons of agave
- 1/2 lemon's zest
- 1 sprig of fresh mint, plus more for decoration
- Any fruit you like

Directions

- Add everything to the bowl, excluding the mint garnish. For two hours, cover and leave Fruit should be carefully taken out of the original bowl, leaving the marinade behind, and put in a serving bowl. Enjoy! Add some freshly chopped mint on top.

3. Figs with Yogurt

Ingredients

- 8 ounces of fresh figs cut into thirds,
- 2 cups plain Greek yogurt,
- 3 tbsp of honey
- 1/4 cup chopped pistachios A dash of cinnamon powder

Directions

- Heat 1 tablespoon of honey in a medium skillet over medium heat for 1 to 2 minutes, or until warm After adding, sauté the figs with the cut sides down for about 5 minutes, or until they are caramelized.
- Turn off the heat and let stand for two to three minutes. Place the caramelized figs on top of the yogurt after dividing it among serving bowls. Garnish with cinnamon and pistachios. Finish by drizzling the dish with the remaining honey.

4. Vegan Banana Overnight Oats

Ingredients

- 1 cup gluten-free rolled oats Chia seeds, 1 1/2 tbsp.
- 2 tbsp cocoa powder 2 dates with pits
- 1/2 cup espresso
- Almond milk, 1/4 cup one banana
- A dash of salt

Directions

- Include a banana, dates, coffee, almond milk, cocoa powder, and salt in the Blending until smooth in a blender. Place the glass jar with the blended banana mixture inside. Fill the jar with the chia seeds and oats, and then thoroughly stir everything. Cover the jar with a lid and put it in the fridge for the night. Stir thoroughly and serve.

5. Avocado Toast

Ingredients

- One large avocado, peeled, pitted, and roughly chopped
- 1/4 teaspoon of lemon juice, fresh
- 2 tablespoons of finely chopped fresh mint leaves if needed, salt and freshly ground black pepper
- 4 big pieces of rye bread
- 4 sliced and peeled hard-boiled eggs 2 teaspoons of crumbled feta cheese

Directions

- Place the avocado in a bowl and roughly mash with a fork. After thoroughly combining, add the lemon juice, mint, salt, and black pepper. Set aside. Place a nonstick frying pan over medium-high heat, add the slice, and toast it for two minutes on each side.
- Carry out step 4 with the remaining slices. Evenly distribute the avocado mixture over each slice. Top with feta and serve right away.

6. Watermelon Gazpacho served cold

This chilled watermelon gazpacho is a tasty riff on the classic tomato gazpacho that is sweet and filling.

Ingredients

- 6 cups chopped seedless watermelon
- 2 large diced seedless cucumbers
- 2 chopped green onions
- ½ cup river wine garlic
- fresh cilantro leaves in 1/4 cup
- oil of olives, 1 tablespoon
- fresh mint leaves, 3 tablespoons
- 1/4 cup chopped for garnish

Directions

- All the ingredients should be combined in a sizable mixing dish. Combine everything thoroughly, cover, and chill for two hours. Use the back of the wooden spoon to mash the watermelon, and then serve it chilled.

7. Cakes with chocolate chips

Everyone in your family, vegetarian or not, can enjoy chocolate chip pancakes. The batter remaining from this recipe can be stored in the refrigerator and eaten during the remainder of the week.

Ingredients

- one ounce of skim milk
- 2 tablespoons of melted butter
- 1 large beaten egg
- flour, all-purpose, 1 cup
- 2 tablespoons of sugar granulated
- 2 tablespoons of baking powder
- jar of salt
- mini chocolate chips, 1/2 cup

Directions

- In a mixing bowl, combine the milk, butter, & egg. Add the flour, sweetener, baking powder, and salt to the milk mixture after combining them in a separate basin.
- A sizable nonstick skillet should be heated to medium. 3 to 4 tablespoons of batter should be added to the griddle for each pancake. For each pancake, add 1 to 2 teaspoons of small chocolate chips to the wet batter.
- Using a plastic spatula, gently turn the pancakes once bubbles have formed on the surface of the batter. About 1 minute extra of cooking is needed to brown the underside of the pancakes. Repeat with remaining batter after transferring the pancakes to a platter. If preferred, drizzle hot dishes with maple syrup.

8. Raw Mixed Berry Pie

Berries are a great source of vitamin C, and boiling them in this recipe does not degrade their nutritious worth. This pie is natural and wonderful because it only uses ripe berries' natural flavor.

Ingredients

- 2 1/2 pounds coppered walnuts
- (7) apricots
- 1 1/3 cup unsweetened shredded coconut
- ½ cup recent lime juice
- an ounce of raw honey
- sliced and peeled 1 ripe kiwi
- sliced strawberries in 2 cupsups
- a half cup of fresh blueberries
- fresh raspberries, 1/2 cup

Directions

- Place the walnuts & apricots in separate dishes, cover with water, let soak for up to 24 hours. In a food processor, combine the moistened walnuts, apricots, and coconut; process until completely smooth.
- Blend in the lime juice, honey, and kiwi after which, if necessary, add a little water from the apricot soak. Fresh berries should be placed on top after pressing the mixture into a pie plate's bottom.

9. Sweet Peach Jam

Ingredients

- 1 1/2 pounds of pitted and diced fresh peaches
- 1/2 tablespoon vanilla
- 25% of maple syrup

Directions

- Stir well after adding each ingredient to the instant pot. Cover the saucepan with a lid and heat it for one minute. Once finished, permit pressure to escape normally. Open the lid.
- Cook jam until it thickened for 15 minutes with the pot on the sauté setting. Place the container in the refrigerator after pouring it.

10. Warm Peach Compote

Ingredients

- Peeled and chopped 4 peaches,
- 1 tablespoon water
- 1 teaspoon vanilla,
- 1/2 tbsp cornstarch

Directions

- Peaches, vanilla, and water should be added to the instant pot. Cover the saucepan with a lid and heat it for one minute. Once finished, permit pressure to escape normally. Open the lid.
- 1 tablespoon of water and cornstarch should be whisked together in a small bowl before being added to the pot and thoroughly mixed. Enjoy after serving.

11. Pear Sauce

Ingredients

- 8 pears, chopped and coring
- Ground cinnamon 1/2 tsp.
- Ground nutmeg, 1/4 teaspoon
- water, 1 cup

Directions

- Stir well after adding each ingredient to the instant pot. Put a lid on the pot, choose the slow cook setting, and cook on low for 6 hours. Use a potato masher to mash the sauce. Place the container in the refrigerator after pouring it.

12. Raisin Pecan Baked Apples

Ingredients

- 1 cup of red wine, 6 cored and wedged apples
- chopped 1/4 cup pecans 1/4 cup raisins
- 1/3 cup honey
- 1/4 tsp. nutmeg
- 1 tsp. cinnamon
- Few dry fruits any

Directions

- Stir well after adding each ingredient to the instant pot. Cook for 4 minutes on high while covering the vessel with a lid.
- Once finished, allow pressure to drop naturally for 10 minutes before using a fast release to the residual pressure. Open the lid. Stir thoroughly, then plate.

13. Mediterranean Watermelon Salad

Ingredients

- 6 cups of torn mixed salad greens
- 3 cups seeded and diced watermelon
- 12 cups sliced onion
- Extra virgin olive oil, 1 tablespoon
- 1/3 cup crumbled feta cheese ground black pepper

Directions

- Combine all ingredients in a large bowl. Toss everything together. Prior to serving, allow chilling.

14. Lychee and Pomegranate Sorbet

Ingredients

- 1/4 cup cubes of dragon fruit
- 8 pitted and peeled lychees Lemon juice from one
- stevia sugar, 3 tablespoons
- Pomegranate seeds, 2 tablespoons

Directions

- Combine the dragon fruit, lychees, lemon, and stevia sugar in a blender. Till smooth, pulse. Place the mixture in a jar with a lid and in the refrigerator.

- Give the sorbet at least eight hours to harden. Before serving, top with pomegranate seeds.

15. Blueberry Coconut Energy Bites

Ingredients

- 1 cup rolled old-fashioned oats (or gluten-free oats)
- Ground flaxseed meal, 1/4 cup
- Chia seeds, 2 tablespoons
- 1/8 teaspoon of cinnamon powder
- a dash of salt, the sea

- One-half cup of creamy almond butter
- Honey, 1/4 cup
- One-half teaspoon of vanilla extract
- optional 1/2 tsp coconut extract
- A quarter cup of dried blueberries
- 14 cups of sweetened coconut flakes

Instructions

- Oats, ground chia seeds, flax seeds, cinnamon, and salt should all be combined in a big dish. Put the almond butter in a tiny bowl that can go in the microwave. Microwave for 20 to 30 seconds, or until just melted until smooth, and stir.
- Melted almond butter should be combined with honey, vanilla, and coconut extract if used. Until smooth, stir Pour over and blend thoroughly with the oat mixture. Add the coconut and dried blueberries after mixing.
- Make little balls out of the mixture, using 1-2 tablespoons for each ball. Put in an airtight container, then store in the fridge for up to two weeks. The balls can also be stored in the freezer for up to a month.

Chapter 9
28 Days Meal Plan

Week 1

Monday
Breakfast: Slow Cooker Mediterranean Frittata
Lunch: Greek sheet pan chicken
Snack: Avocado Toast
Dinner: Mediterranean Chicken and Rice

Tuesday
Breakfast: Blueberry Smoothie Bowl
Lunch: Moroccan Lamb Stew
Snack: Cakes with chocolate chips
Dinner: Tomato Brown Rice Pilaf

Wednesday
Breakfast: Mediterranean Egg Muffins with Ham
Lunch: Mediterranean Baked Zucchini Sticks
Snack: Raw Mixed Berry Pie
Dinner: Greek Lamb Chops

Thursday
Breakfast: Feta Frozen Yogurt
Lunch: Lentil Greek Salad
Snack: Raisin Pecan Baked Apples
Dinner: Monkfish stuffed

Friday
Breakfast: Pan Con Tomato
Lunch: Chicken Salad Panini Sandwiches
Snack: Pear Sauce
Dinner: Spicy Crab Pasta

Saturday
Breakfast: Mediterranean Toast
Lunch: Greek Style Chicken Salad
Snack: Raw Mixed Berry Pie
Dinner: Greek Lemon Chicken and Potatoes

Sunday
Breakfast: Chia and Berry Overnight Oats
Lunch: Chicken and Mozzarella Melts
Snack: Watermelon Gazpacho
Dinner: Salmon and Couscous Casserole

Week 2

Monday
Breakfast: Traditional Italian Biscotti
Lunch: Zucchini and Lemon Noodles
Snack: Warm Peach Compote
Dinner: Lentil Soup

Tuesday

Breakfast: Date and Almond Smoothie

Lunch: Falafel Burger

Snack: Lychee and Pomegranate Sorbet

Dinner: Greek Lemon Chicken Soup

Wednesday

Breakfast: Mediterranean Omelet

Lunch: White Bean Salad with Tomato & Cucumber

Snack: Frozen Fruit Salad with Mint

Dinner: Lemon Pepper Salmon

Thursday

Breakfast: Egg White Scramble with Veggies

Lunch: Pita Bread, Hummus, and Greek Salad

Snack: Blueberry Coconut Energy Bites

Dinner: Parmesan and Lemon Chicken with Zucchini Noodles

Friday

Breakfast: Herb and Egg Frittata

Lunch: Mediterranean Salad Bowl

Snack: Raisin Pecan Baked Apples

Dinner: Garlic Shrimp

Saturday

Breakfast: Multi Grain Breakfast Sandwich

Lunch: Shrimp Tortilla

Snack: Vegan Banana Overnight Oats

Dinner: Shrimp Scampi Skewers

Sunday

Breakfast: Oats with Fruit

Lunch: Mediterranean Tuna Salad

Snack: Raisin Pecan Baked Apples

Dinner: Kale and Feta Pasta

Week 3

Monday

Breakfast: Traditional Italian Biscotti

Lunch: Lentil, Shrimp and Bean Salad

Snack: Vegan Banana Overnight Oats

Dinner: Mediterranean Veggie Chicken

Tuesday

Breakfast: Strawberry-Rhubarb Smoothie

Lunch: Mediterranean Tomato Salad with Fresh Herbs

Snack: Warm Peach Compote

Dinner: Lentil Soup

Wednesday

Breakfast: Pumpkin-Gingerbread Smoothie

Lunch: Shrimp Avocado Garlic Bread

Snack: Lychee and Pomegranate Sorbet

Dinner: Risotto with Mushrooms

Thursday

Breakfast: Barley Porridge

Lunch: Quinoa Veggie Wrap

Snack: Figs with Yogurt

Dinner: Zoodles with Avocado and Mango Sauce

Friday

Breakfast: Bircher Muesli

Lunch: Green Bowl with Chicken and Herbs

Snack: Mediterranean Watermelon Salad

Dinner: Steamed Mussels

Saturday

Breakfast: Zucchini Fritters (Ejjeh)

Lunch: Chicken Noodle Soup

Snack: Avocado Apple Breakfast Smoothie

Dinner: One Skillet of Mediterranean Chicken with Tomatoes

Sunday

Breakfast: Spiced Almond Pancakes

Lunch: Slow-roasted Mediterranean lamb

Snack: Figs with Yogurt

Dinner: One Pan of Mediterranean Chicken Orzo

Week 4

Monday

Breakfast: Hearty Pear and Mango Smoothie

Lunch: Favorite Pepper Soup

Snack: Cakes with chocolate chips

Dinner: Homemade Hummus with Perky Pesto & Crumbly Cheese

Tuesday

Breakfast: Lovely Eggplant Salad

Lunch: The Mediterranean Tomato Soup

Snack: Blueberry Coconut Energy Bites

Dinner: Minty Melon & Fruity Feta with Cool Cucumber

Wednesday

Breakfast: Lovely Artichoke Frittata

Lunch: Authentic Yogurt and Cucumber Salad

Snack: Cakes with chocolate chips

Dinner: Lemony Steamed Asparagus with Cheese Chips

Thursday

Breakfast: Full Eggs in a Squash

Lunch: Delightful Pesto Pizza

Snack: Mediterranean Watermelon Salad

Dinner: Mediterranean Minestrone

Friday

Breakfast: The Great Barley Porridge

Lunch: Linguine Dredged in Tomato Clam Sauce

Snack: Avocado Apple Breakfast Smoothie

Dinner: Oven-grilled Oyster Mushroom Meal

Saturday

Breakfast: Cool Tomato and Dill Frittata

Lunch: Wild Mushrooms and Pork Chops

Snack: Frozen Fruit Salad with Mint

Dinner: Zestful Zucchini & Dough Dumplings (Gnocchi)

Sunday

Breakfast: Hearty Strawberry and Rhubarb Smoothie

Lunch: Mediterranean Lamb Chops

Snack: Raisin Pecan Baked Apples

Dinner: Verdant Veggie Crispy Cakes

Index

Recipes

Conclusion

The Mediterranean diet is both tasty and nourishing since it is full of rich components including fruits, veggies, whole grains, and heart-healthy fats. It's also linked to several advantages, including those that may boost brain function, advance heart health, control blood sugar levels, and more.

There are numerous broad suggestions you can follow to incorporate the tenets of the diet into your daily routine, even if there are no specific directions for how to follow the Mediterranean diet. The Mediterranean diet has constantly ranked first among the healthiest weight loss diets since it is not only very healthy, but it can also be adopted as a lifestyle for the rest of your life to "cement" its advantages.

This book is a terrific resource for you if you're feeling stuck and helpless about your general health. It will inspire and motivate you to make positive changes in your life by following the Mediterranean diet. If you've made the decision to start living a healthy life as a result of being inspired by one of the oldest diets in history, then don't wait to begin getting assistance from here and move forward!

Hopefully, this guide helped you to get a clear concept about the topic and will provide you assistance whenever you need that! Feel free to read it again anytime whenever you get distracted and implement it practically to get positive outcomes.

66086093R00072